A WORD TO THE WISE

A WORD TO THE WISE

Lessons from Proverbs for Young Adults

BRANDON COOPER

A Word to the Wise

Published by
Deep River Books
Sisters, Oregon
www.deepriverbooks.com

ISBN: 1-935265-25-3
ISBN: 978-1-935265-25-2

Library of Congress: 2010926498

Printed in the USA

Cover design by Robin Black

To my dear wife, Amy,
who exemplifies the excellent wife
of Proverbs 31

and

To my students at El Camino Academy,
whose keen minds and thirsty souls in class
provided much of the discussion
that shaped this book.

Soli deo gloria.

Table of Contents

ACKNOWLEDGMENTS

I am deeply indebted to a number of people for their help on this project. I would like to thank the faculty of Trinity Evangelical Divinity School, especially John Nyquist, Greg Scharf, and Dennis Magary, for the training I received in studying and proclaiming God's Word. If I have correctly handled the word of truth, it is largely a testimony to their faithfulness as teachers of the Word. I am also grateful for the encouragement and support of the staff, student body, and community of El Camino Academy. Special thanks to Heather Cooper, Jennifer Johnson, and Kay Coulter, who proved invaluable in the editing process, and to Lacey Ogle and the whole VMI team.

Finally, I would like to thank my darling wife, Amy, whose love and support sustain me through the most trying ministry times and constantly challenge my soul. Apart from Christ himself and the grace I know in him, you are the greatest gift I have received from the Giver of all good gifts.

ONE

WHY PROVERBS?

Introduction

A fair question to ask before devoting time to studying any book is, "Why bother?" What makes this one worth studying to the neglect of any other? Now, when it comes to studying the Bible, at least we know why that book is worth studying, as it is the only one that is God's revelation to humanity. But even within the Bible we can still ask why this part and not another? Why Proverbs, say, and not Romans? Well, I hope that you will study Romans too—and every book of the Bible—because every part has something to say to us today. But I believe that Proverbs is a particularly good book to study as a young adult—heading into high school or college—because it addresses the same issues that young adults face today: love and sex, friendship (how to be a good friend, how to choose friends), making decisions (like where to go to college, what career to pursue), and laziness (ever heard of senioritis?).

Not only does it address the hot issues of this stage of your life, but it even seems to address these issues in the lives of youth. In Proverbs 1:4, the writer specifies that these words are for giving knowledge to the *young*. Much of the wisdom contained in Proverbs will best help someone who is just beginning to face life's major decisions. A close study of Proverbs will help prepare you to make the wise choices early, before it's too late.

I hope this explains why Proverbs will prove such a valuable book to study at this time in your life. I fully believe that if you commit to a careful reading of Proverbs, you will find yourself wiser and godlier than you would have been if you hadn't read it. With that in mind, let's take a quick look at the introduction to the book, Proverbs 1:1–7.

The Starting Point

"The fear of the LORD is the beginning of knowledge" (Proverbs 1:7). This short phrase, which occurs several times in the book of Proverbs, really sums up the whole book. We could almost think of it as the motto—the theme statement—for the whole book. So what does this important statement teach?

First, we need to understand exactly what is meant by "the beginning." Does it refer to time or to importance? That is, do we need the fear of God *first* before we learn anything else, or do we need the fear of God *more importantly* than we need knowledge? I think the answer is both. An illustration may help explain how the two work together. Imagine when you learned to read. If your kindergarten teacher had said, "Letters are the beginning of reading," would she have meant you needed to learn your alphabet *before* you learned to read? Of course. You can't read words without knowing what the letters are. But she probably also meant that the alphabet is the *foundation* or *most important part* of reading. So the fear of the Lord is to knowledge what the alphabet is to reading. You need it first, and it will always be the most important part of wisdom.

Second, what does it mean to *fear* the Lord? In today's usage, "to fear" means to be afraid of or to dread something. Perhaps then the beginning of knowledge is the dread of punishment from God. This is possible, I suppose, especially for a younger believer. Young children often learn "knowledge"—not to cross the street alone, not to touch a hot stove, not to steal toys from other kids—by *fearing* a spanking from their parents. But those kids grow up, and so do we as believers. Later, we learn knowledge—don't smoke, study hard in school, read your Bible—by *respecting* what other people teach us: our parents, our pastors, our friends. With this in mind, to *fear the Lord* would mean *to revere God*, to give him respect and awe as we follow him.

So the first and most important thing we must do in order to gain wisdom and knowledge is to revere God. If you get the starting point wrong—

the fear of the Lord—then the whole project goes wrong, and you'll never gain any wisdom. My wife learned this by way of illustration when she was a high school student on a short-term mission trip to Venezuela. She and her youth group were building adobe huts for a poor village that had been devastated by flooding a few months before. The team quickly learned that if they laid the foundation to the hut incorrectly, the rest of the hut would never quite fit together right—corners wouldn't match up, bricks wouldn't fit, and the like. In the same way, beginning to seek knowledge without first fearing God will leave your life a misshapen hut.

Five Reasons to Read Proverbs

In the first seven verses, Proverbs gives us an introduction to the whole book, a preamble. (Think of the Constitution: "We the people. . . ." The preamble tells us the reason why the document was written and what value it has.) We have already seen what verse 7 means. But in verses 1–6, Proverbs lists five reasons why these proverbs are worth studying. Understanding these five reasons will help us persist in studying the book, knowing that it will benefit us in very specific ways. Here are verses 1–6:

> The proverbs of Solomon son of David, king of Israel:
> for attaining wisdom and discipline;
> for understanding words of insight;
> for acquiring a disciplined and prudent life,
> doing what is right and just and fair;
> for giving prudence to the simple,
> knowledge and discretion to the young—
> let the wise listen and add to their learning,
> and let the discerning get guidance—
> for understanding proverbs and parables,
> the sayings and riddles of the wise.

You may have noticed that one word keeps coming up in this list: for. The Proverbs are "*for* attaining wisdom," "*for* understanding words of insight," "*for* acquiring a disciplined life," "*for* giving prudence," and "*for* understanding." The repetition of the word "for" marks off the five reasons why it is worth studying the book of Proverbs. Let's take a quick look at each reason individually.

First, the proverbs are *for attaining wisdom and discipline*. That is, if you study the proverbs carefully, you will eventually receive the instruction you need to live your life well. We may think of the difference between wisdom and discipline as the difference between practical instruction (what you need to know to make life work) and ethical instruction (your moral responsibility as a follower of God). If you study the proverbs, you will grow in this type of knowledge.

Second, the proverbs are *for understanding words of insight*. Not only will you get wisdom, but you will understand it. Sometimes a person can learn *about* a subject without ever really understanding it. For me, chemistry falls into this category. I took two years of it in high school and couldn't tell you a thing about it. But here we are promised that if we study the proverbs, we will really understand wisdom.

Third, the proverbs are *for acquiring a disciplined and prudent life, doing what is right and just and fair.* Studying the proverbs will help us learn what it means to be wise and ethical, and the writer then lets us know exactly what it means to be wise and ethical. A disciplined and prudent life means *doing what is right and just and fair*. The wise person works at those characteristics that are essential for a society to function well: righteousness (an individual doing what is right), justice (a society doing what is right), and equality (which here actually refers to honest speech and judgment). The proverbs will help us learn not only what we need to do to fear God, but what society needs to do to fear God also. Now, Proverbs was written to Israel, a theocracy (a government in which God rules directly), whereas none of us lives in a theocracy today. So society will probably not look the way Proverbs envisions. But we as Christians can work to make sure justice and honesty are values that are evident in our society.

Fourth, the proverbs are *for giving prudence to the simple, knowledge and discretion to the young*. The last three promises have all described what *we* will be able to do if we study the proverbs. But this promise tells us what *the book* will do for us if we study it. We are all "simple" (that is, we don't know everything there is to know about how life should work), and some of us are still young. I am only 28, so I would like to think of myself as still being young. Being simple and young means that we could all stand to learn a little bit more. And if we study the proverbs, we will! That is what the book promises to do for us.

Fifth, the proverbs are *for understanding proverbs and parables, the sayings and riddles of the wise*. This is another promise about what we, the readers, will be able to do if we study the proverbs. Basically, the more you read them, the better you get at reading them. Proverbs are a little bit tricky—they're meant to be compact and clever—but with practice, you'll be able to understand them more and more. So the good news is that it gets easier.

But What about Us?

You may have noticed that I skipped a part of verses 2–6 when I was giving the five reasons to study the proverbs. That was verse 5: "Let the wise listen and add to their learning, and let the discerning get guidance." The book promises to do a lot for us if we will study it: we'll learn wisdom and ethics, justice, righteousness, and equality; we'll get better and better at reading, and so on. But all of that hinges on us: *if* we study it. In other words, sleeping with the book under our pillows won't do us a bit of good. We need to knuckle down and do the hard work of trying to learn what the book wants to teach us. We need to *listen* to what the book says and *add* it to what we know (or think we know). And we need to *get*—to receive—the guidance and instruction that the book offers.

If you are willing to take that step—and I hope you are—then Proverbs promises to change your life, really and truly. The wisdom contained within this book is a treasure chest waiting to be opened by any who would draw closer to God.

Memory Verse

At the end of each chapter, I will provide you with a verse that you may wish to memorize. Memorizing scripture can be difficult, but it is extraordinarily valuable. As Proverbs says, "If you...store up my commands within you... then you will understand the fear of the LORD and find the knowledge of God" (Proverbs 2:1, 5). Will you commit to storing up God's commands within you?

Memory Verse

"The fear of the Lord is the beginning of knowledge, but fools despise wisdom and discipline."
Proverbs 1:7

Study Questions

1. Why do you want to study Proverbs?

2. What does it mean that "the fear of the LORD is the beginning of knowledge"?

3. How does the fear of God affect how we gain knowledge? Give an example.

4. What does Proverbs promise to do for us? What do we need to do?

5. Will you commit to learning from the book of Proverbs—listening to it, adding to your knowledge, getting guidance from it?

TWO

Seeking Wisdom

Seeking What Is Valuable

My wife and I are missionaries in Bogotá, Colombia. We love it here—the people, the sights, the food. But sometimes we miss what we knew back home, especially the food. Because we live in a big city, we can sometimes find the food we miss most from the States—tacos, ice cream, or whatever. The tricky part is knowing where to look—which store, which aisle, which shelf. But because we like the food so much, we are willing to spend a little extra time looking around for it. We might even try a different grocery store just to see if they have something we can't find at our usual store.

I think this holds true for most people: we are willing to spend the time *seeking* what is most *valuable* to us. Perhaps you spend time seeking just the right pair of jeans or shirt. Or maybe you exert a little extra effort looking for a good video game or book to read. Whatever matters most to you, I bet you're willing to look for it.

So what does any of this have to do with Proverbs? The question is does wisdom matter enough for us to "waste time" seeking it?

The Value of Wisdom

The book of Proverbs tells us that wisdom has tremendous value, and so we should seek it with all of the energy we can muster. The first few verses of chapter two give us some insight into how valuable wisdom is.

My son, if you accept my words
and store up my commands within you,
turning your ear to wisdom
and applying your heart to understanding,
and if you call out for insight
and cry aloud for understanding,
and if you look for it as for silver
and search for it as for hidden treasure,
then you will understand the fear of the LORD
and find the knowledge of God.

PROVERBS 2:1–5

Notice that the writer compares wisdom to silver and hidden treasure in these verses. If someone told you that a million dollars—even a thousand dollars—worth of silver was buried in your backyard, wouldn't you invest a little time trying to find where? Here Proverbs tells us to look for wisdom in the same way. It is as valuable as precious metal, so spend some time looking for it. If you do, then you will be well on your way to accomplishing the motto of Proverbs: "The fear of the LORD is the beginning of knowledge." If you search for wisdom as for hidden treasure, you will *understand the fear of the Lord* and that, as we saw in the last chapter, leads to the *knowledge of God.* And the writer even lets us know how we can go about seeking wisdom: "accept my words," "store up my commands," "turn your ear to wisdom," "apply your heart to understanding." In order to find wisdom, we need to listen to the words and commands of the saints who have gone before us—Solomon, Lemuel, Agur, the wise (all of whom helped write Proverbs). And we need to be single-minded in our pursuit of wisdom—we need to commit to studying wisdom, reading insights, listening to understanding. That is the purpose of this book—to provide you with a brief guided tour of the wisdom of Proverbs as it relates to your life today.

Comparing wisdom to silver and hidden treasure is good, but if you're like me, you want to know *why* wisdom is so valuable. What makes it better than money? (We'll talk about money later on.) Listen to what Proverbs 4:6–9 has to say about that:

Do not forsake wisdom, and she will protect you;
love her, and she will watch over you.
Wisdom is supreme; therefore get wisdom.
Though it cost all you have, get understanding.
Esteem her, and she will exalt you;
embrace her, and she will honor you.
She will set a garland of grace on your head
and present you with a crown of splendor.

Here the writer says that it would be worth it to spend all the money you have *in order to get wisdom*. "Though it cost you all you have, get understanding." That is a remarkable statement. I don't know of many people who would be willing to bankrupt themselves in pursuit of a true understanding of the world, but that is exactly what Proverbs tells us we should be willing to do. Why? Because of what wisdom will do for you. She will *protect* you, *watch over* you, *exalt* you, and *honor* you. And in the end, you get a crown of splendor from her. Not bad. Now, I'm not so sure that wisdom will appear in bodily form to place the crown on your head. Rather, if you become a wise person, you will soon find that the wisdom you possess will keep you from getting into trouble—with the opposite sex, for example—and in that way "wisdom" will protect you. If you become a wise person, people will come to you for godly advice, and when you give it, they will respect you—and in that way "wisdom" will honor and exalt you. Wisdom is so valuable because of the value of becoming a *wise person*—what it will mean for your character, your relationships, your life.

Truly, "How much better to get wisdom than gold, to choose understanding rather than silver!" (Proverbs 16:16).

The Character of Wisdom

So we have seen that wisdom is worth seeking. But more remarkably, wisdom *seeks us*. "Does not wisdom call out? Does not understanding raise her voice?" (Proverbs 8:1). Indeed she does. She calls aloud from the highest point in the city (Proverbs 9:3). Interestingly, the highest point in the city was the place where the gods of that city lived—and in Jerusalem, where the temple of the Lord was located. In other words, wisdom dwells with God. (For this reason, some have connected wisdom with the Holy Spirit, the third member of the Trinity.) From this place, she cries out so that all can hear her:

To you, O men, I call out;
    I raise my voice to all mankind.
You who are simple, gain prudence;
    you who are foolish,
gain understanding.
    Listen, for I have worthy things to say;
I open my lips to speak what is right."

PROVERBS 8:4–6

Wisdom wishes to be found, and makes herself available to any who learn from her. "I love those who love me, and those who seek me find me" (Proverbs 8:17). She waits for all of us with open arms, ready and willing to teach us if only we will come and listen.

Two Women

Unfortunately, wisdom is not the only one who calls to us. Folly—her competition for the hearts of men—also woos humanity to come and learn what she has to teach. "'Let all who are simple come in here!' / she says to those who lack judgment. / 'Stolen water is sweet; / food eaten in secret is delicious!'" (Proverbs 9:16–17). In Proverbs, to be a fool is not just to be silly or unintelligent, but to be immoral—to choose to go against God's will for your life. This is why she wants us to drink "stolen" water and to eat food in "secret." (In this case, these are both probably euphemisms for illicit sex.)

We have two people calling out to us—Wisdom and Folly. Now, the first nine chapters of Proverbs are addressed to "my son" (for example, Proverbs 1:8). So it makes sense that the father figure would illustrate the choice his "son" has to make by way of prospective girlfriends. If you're a girl reading this, feel free to imagine instead that Wisdom and Folly are good-looking guys looking to date you.

In any case, we have these two women—Miss Wisdom and Miss Folly (she'd probably prefer to think of herself as "Miss Thang"). Both are calling out to you, both want to get to know you better. It is always nice when someone likes you, so you're feeling pretty good about yourself. You must be pretty popular. How do you choose between the two? You can only ask one to the prom, so you've got to make a choice. Who is it going to be?

Well, maybe you start writing out a list of pros and cons for both. Since wisdom and folly aren't real people, you can't really decide based on looks or personality. We will have to look elsewhere for the deciding factor. Here is a possibility: what will each one do for you? Will she make your life richer and better, or worse?

We have already seen that wisdom will improve your life—she will exalt and honor you, protect and watch over you. Not bad. How about folly?

Proverbs describes folly as being like an adulteress—someone who calls men to perverse pleasure that will eventually end in their ruin. Proverbs says of those who listen to folly, "But little do they know that the dead are there, that her guests are in the depths of the grave" (Proverbs 9:18). In other words, folly promises a good time to any who would come to her, but in the end, she ruins people's lives, sending them to an early death.

Two Paths

We see in the contrast between wisdom and folly the choice we have—to follow wisdom or to follow folly. There are two possible paths that we can take, two roads that lead in very different directions. On the one hand, we can follow wisdom, begin with the fear of the Lord, and eventually find ourselves in the New Jerusalem, the heavenly city where God himself will dwell. Of the person who chooses this path Proverbs says, "He who gets wisdom loves his own soul; he who cherishes understanding prospers" (Proverbs 19:8).

On the other hand, we can follow folly, make foolish and rash choices.

Where does that lead? Well, "Her house is a highway to the grave, leading down to the chambers of death" (Proverbs 7:27). Tough choice.

Memory Verse

*"Wisdom is supreme; therefore get wisdom.
Though it cost all you have, get understanding."*
Proverbs 4:7

Study Questions

1. What do you "spend time looking for"? What matters most to you?

2. How can you commit to pursuing wisdom?

3. In what ways could wisdom protect and honor you if you seek her?

4. How have you seen the difference between wisdom and folly in your own life?

5. Have you ever seen folly lead to some sort of spiritual or emotional death? What were the circumstances?

THREE

Making Decisions

We saw in the last chapter that there are two paths before us—the way of wisdom and the way of folly. We saw that choosing wisdom will lead to our honor and protection, whereas choosing folly ends in death. I hope by now you have seen the value of seeking wisdom—the choice seems easy enough on the broad scale. But here's the problem: we don't get to choose one path or the other and then call it quits for the rest of our lives. You don't come to a fork in the road, take the right fork, and never have to worry about the left fork again. Rather, we have to make the choice *over and over again* to do what is wise instead of what is foolish. At any moment—when facing any decision of consequence—we can mistakenly choose the wrong path. "There is a way that seems right to a man, but in the end it leads to death" (Proverbs 14:12).

In this chapter, we will look at some ways to avoid making the wrong choice when facing major (and minor) life decisions. The first two—accepting instruction and listening to advice—are closely related. "Listen to advice and accept instruction, and in the end you will be wise" (Proverbs 19:20).

Accepting Instruction

In order to be wise, one must accept instruction. The word for "instruction" could also be translated "discipline." In other words, "instruction" refers to the moral commands that are given to you by God, parents, or other authority figures. It can refer to punishment if a poor choice was made; but here I think it refers to the warnings that are given to prevent you from making poor choices—"don't do drugs," "pay attention in school," or something like that. So the translation "instruction" probably makes good sense. Instruction, then, is *unsolicited advice*—advice given to you whether you wanted to hear it or not.

Proverbs teaches us that we must *accept instruction* if we want to be wise. Being wise, as we have seen, means being protected and watched over, exalted and honored (Proverbs 4:6–9). How instruction functions to achieve this should be clear: the instruction that we are given that is negative—"*don't* do drugs," "*don't* have sex before marriage"—protects us, watches over us. These negative commands keep us from making the types of choices that can greatly harm our lives. A person who engages in promiscuous sex, for example, may end up with a sexually transmitted disease, and may die young or suffer physically for some time.

On the other hand, the instruction that we are given that is positive—"*Do* pay attention in school," "*Do* read your Bible everyday"—exalts and honors us. These positive commands help us make the types of choices that will benefit us in life. Someone who studies hard in school, for example, may get into a better college and eventually work at a high-paying job.

Elsewhere in Proverbs we learn this same lesson. Proverbs 13:13 says, "He who scorns instruction will pay for it, but he who respects a command is rewarded." If you reject the instruction that your parents or pastors give to you, you will pay for it; but if you listen to the command—respect it as being wise and valuable, it will pay you (you'll get rewarded). We have here the same two paths we talked about in the last chapter: with every decision you face, you can choose to listen to instruction, and prosper, or you can choose to reject it—to follow folly—and so end up suffering as a result.

Remember, "Whoever gives heed to instruction prospers, and blessed is he who trusts in the LORD" (Proverbs 16:20). Choosing wisdom—choosing to listen to the unsolicited advice that wise people give you—will be a blessing in your life.

A Test Case: Accepting Instruction

Let's look at a common example to see how accepting instruction will benefit you when making a decision, whereas rejecting it will harm you. Instruction tends to focus on absolutes—those choices that are moral in nature that are always in effect. The Ten Commandments are a good example of instruction, as is Jesus' Sermon on the Mount. So our example will be one of these "absolute" commands.

No doubt you have heard before, "don't drink and drive." This is a good example of instruction. You probably never had to ask your parents, "Should I drink and drive or not?" They had told you long before you would have asked. Your school has probably told you also. My high school had a lengthy presentation the week before prom about what happens to people who drink and drive. We had all gotten the instruction we needed.

So we know the instruction: "Don't drink and drive." Let's look at the two possible responses to the instruction. First, we could be fools and reject the instruction we have been given. Many do this, with tragic consequences. Someone very close to me made this mistake a few years ago. He had been drinking heavily and then tried to drive himself home. He crashed himself into a telephone pole, breaking his nose very badly and totaling the car. He felt fortunate, as he very well could have killed himself. Many others are not so lucky. They do kill themselves, or worse yet, kill someone else. Almost everyone knows someone whose life has been affected by a drunk driver. Those who scorn instruction pay for it—with legal consequences (losing a license, going to jail) or worse.

But there is another possible response. We can accept the instruction as being good and wise and listen to it. What are the consequences? None. That's the good news, because with drinking and driving, the only possible consequences are bad ones. Wisdom has protected us, has watched over us, and we have escaped terrible consequences simply by accepting instruction. Accepting instruction will help us to make better choices, as will listening to the advice of godly people.

Listening to Advice

Instruction, as I said, refers to *unsolicited advice*, the stuff people tell you even when you don't want to hear it. Advice, on the other hand, refers to *solicited advice*—when you ask someone wise to give you his or her opinion on what decision to make. Proverbs makes it clear that we should listen to instruction when given by godly people; but Proverbs also teaches us that we should ask wise people to give us their advice when we don't know what to do or when facing a major decision.

Humans tend to be self-sufficient, or so we think. And so, when faced with a major choice, many will weigh the options by themselves, without seeking help from a trusted friend or relative. But this doesn't make much sense. Why cut yourself off from a wealth of accumulated wisdom—people who have been where you are and know how the decision may affect you later in life? Proverbs 20:18 says, "Make plans by seeking advice; if you wage war, obtain guidance." Whatever plans you make—where to go to college, what to do as a career, even whom to date—*seek advice*. Ask godly, mature people to see what they think about the matter. They may have some profound insight that you would never have considered. I chose to go to the college that I went to largely because I asked a lot of people what they thought about a certain issue (a secular or Christian school), and then *listened* to what they had to say. And I am grateful for their advice, as I think I went to the right school for me.

When you face any major decision—like a king waging war—it would be nothing short of foolishness to ignore what others think. A king who didn't seek advice before waging war would very likely lose that war. "Plans fail for lack of counsel, but with many advisers they succeed" (Proverbs 15:22). If you have to make a big choice, *obtain guidance*, get some advisers so that you know your plans will work. Go out and *find someone* to help you. "The discerning heart seeks knowledge, but the mouth of a fool feeds on folly" (Proverbs 15:14). Wise people don't just listen to advice, they *seek* it. Many people will not offer advice unless you ask because they don't want to seem nosy. So make sure that you ask them what they think. But make sure that you seek knowledge and not folly.

Seeking advice is very important, but you've got to make sure that it is good advice. A wise person seeks knowledge, but a *fool feeds on folly*. Both types of people seek advice, but only the former seeks *good* advice. This part may sound a little hard, but I've got to say it. Oftentimes, *your friends will not be the best people to give you advice*.

Now I have no doubt that your friends are very good people who want the best for you, but the plain fact of the matter is that they are in the exact same stage of life as you. You will lose the benefit of hindsight—of someone being able to look back on mistakes and successes and learn from them—if you ask people who have not had to make that decision yet. A junior in high school probably doesn't know much about selecting a college, whereas those who have graduated from college will know if the process they used works.

This brings up a related point. When seeking advice, be sure to seek it from someone who is really wise. Wisdom and folly are not just intellectual categories, they are *moral* categories. Wise people seek to please God, whereas fools seek to please themselves. In the language of Proverbs, listening to fools is the same as listening to wicked people. And, "The plans of the righteous are just, but the advice of the wicked is deceitful" (Proverbs 12:5). Seeking advice from fools—from wicked people—will not help you at all. It will hurt you. The advice will be *deceitful*. Either the person will intentionally try to deceive you (not as likely) or the person will accidentally try to deceive you—by giving advice that he or she thinks is good, but which is in reality evil.

I experienced this firsthand. When I was a teenager, I can remember an older friend (not a Christian) telling me that I should have sex before I was married. He thought that the best way to love your wife was to make sure you were as good in bed as possible, and well, practice makes perfect. (We'll talk about how foolish this is when we get to the chapter on sex.) Now, my friend was not *trying* to hurt me, to wreck my marriage before I'd even met my wife, but if I had listened to his advice, that is exactly what would have happened. Make sure you get advice from the right people—wise, mature, and godly people.

Another Test Case: Listening to Advice

Whereas instruction tends to deal with the absolutes, advice deals with those issues that have no clear-cut answer. Choosing a college or career is an excellent example of a decision about which it would be wise to seek advice. There are not really absolutes here: it isn't wrong to go the University of Illinois, or sin not to go to Calvin College. The choice is yours. Perhaps God is leading you in a specific direction, but there is no eleventh commandment, "Thou shalt not attend the University of Southern California." That would be absurd. So how do you decide which college or university to attend, or which career to pursue? Let's focus on the career decision (as that will affect where you go to school anyway).

Choosing a career will likely depend on two main factors: your skills and your interests. You may be very good at science but absolutely hate it, so you probably shouldn't devote your life to it. On the other hand, you may absolutely love music, but can't carry a tune with two hands and a bucket. Probably music theatre should not be in your future (although I've heard some pop stars who challenge this assumption). The wise person will seek advice from people who know him or her, so that they can help evaluate strengths and weaknesses, passion and interest.

My best friend is the choir director at a high school near Chicago. Every year he has to talk with students who have loved being in choir and who want to pursue a career in music. Many of these students are talented and devoted, and several have made excellent music teachers or singers. However, some of the students who express this interest quite frankly lack the necessary talent to succeed in a difficult music industry. Every year he has to advise certain students to consider some other career path. The students who listen to his advice usually discover another interest where there is more skill, and have happy careers in other fields. Others do not listen to him, though, and they end up doing very poorly in college, switching majors late, and starting out in life bitter and hurt. Their plans failed because they did not seek counsel or did not listen to it when it was given. When you make plans, seek advice and follow it if it is good.

The first two keys to making a wise decision involve other people—instruction and advice. The last has to do with you alone: making plans.

Thinking Ahead

One of the keys to making a wise decision is to think ahead—not to get caught up in the moment, but to have a sense of where you're going and how this fits with the bigger picture. Those who plan ahead have a much better chance of accomplishing what they desire. "The plans of the diligent lead to profit as surely as haste leads to poverty" (Proverbs 21:5). In this proverb, the writer considers wealth. Those who plan for their financial future will reap much profit—a good retirement, a stable income, a promotion; however, those who do not plan first but hastily make decisions will end in poverty—taking a job they don't like and so having to switch careers late in life, buying stock on an unreliable tip, or making an expensive purchase instead of saving.

I experienced this when I was in eighth grade. I had been saving up money for some time—Christmas and birthday presents mostly—for no particular reason. I was just saving money so that I would have it later when I needed it. Well, when in eighth grade, I decided to buy an electric guitar, which cost me most of my savings. The problem was, I wasn't very good at guitar and never really bothered to get better. Even today I'm not much of an electric guitar player, even though I play the acoustic guitar frequently. I made a hasty purchase and regretted it later—especially when another purchase opportunity came along that I really wanted to take but now couldn't.

Making plans requires that we think before we act. This is the whole key. Too often we choose before we think, only to regret it later. As the old song says, "Only fools rush in (to love)." Wise people stop and think first. One of my favorite proverbs says, "A simple man believes anything, but a prudent man gives thought to his steps" (Proverbs 14:15). A prudent man—a wise man—*gives thought to his steps*, that is, thinks before he acts. The whole idea of "steps" suggests the image of hiking. When hiking, you have to be careful where you step, or else you could slip and fall. I remember hiking at Cascade Lakes in New York with a friend some years ago. We were coming down the mountain on a particularly steep and rocky part of the trail. My friend stepped carelessly and ended up tumbling down the trail about 200 feet. He ended up suffering only some bad bruising, but he easily could have been killed. We face the same danger—metaphorically speaking—when we make quick decisions without thinking first. Before planting your feet on whatever path you choose, be sure the path won't be the death of you!

I find it interesting that in this proverb the "simple man believes anything." The opposite of thinking before acting is *believing anything*. Whatever someone tells you, that's what you think is true. Imagine if I had been a simpleton when listening to my friend try and talk to me into having premarital sex. Instead, I gave thought to my steps, and am eternally grateful that I did. This can be a tremendous danger for young adults because you are encountering so much new information at school and in life. You may find that you are beginning to be interested in politics, religion (not just Christianity), and current events in a way that you weren't just a few years ago. Probably some adults—perhaps teachers or youth pastors—are influencing your opinion of various issues like global warming, poverty, and religious pluralism (the belief that all religions lead to the same place).

These are tremendously important issues, and I hope you will think a good deal about them. But I hope you will *think* about them, rather than *believing* whatever you are told without weighing the evidence. After all, "It is not good to have zeal without knowledge, nor to be hasty and miss the way" (Proverbs 19:2). I have known many high-school students (and was probably one myself) who were very *zealous* without having much *knowledge* to back it up. It is much wiser to stop and think—read some good books, talk to some people who know—before deciding what stance you will take on some issues. I have been wrestling through some issues—especially poverty—for years now and still haven't fully made up my mind about how I think the government should respond. Take your time, give thought to your steps, and make sure you have the knowledge before the zeal.

Yet Another Test Case: Thinking Ahead

Because I talked a lot about thinking in this section—about politics and religion, for example—I want to consider one of these as a test case. Imagine now that one of your teachers promotes the philosophy known as moral relativism in your class. Moral relativism is the idea that there is no absolute standard of morality, but that we can each choose for ourselves what is right and wrong. (This has probably happened in your class if you attend a public school like I did.)

Simple people will respond by believing their teachers. After all, most teachers are well educated and usually know what they're talking about (though I can think of exceptions). So if this teacher thinks this, why shouldn't you assume it is true? Maybe the teacher has pointed out how arrogant it sounds to assume that somebody—a Christian, perhaps—knows everything about morality. The Bible was written a long time ago and times have changed. Things are different now. Christians should stop judging other people all the time.

You will almost certainly hear comments like this at some point in your life. I've heard them many times. But we want to be wise, and so we give thought to our steps rather than simply believing anything. After all, "The first to present his case seems right, till another comes forward and questions him" (Proverbs 18:17). If you only hear one side of the argument, it seems right; but if you hear the other side, maybe it won't seem quite as strong.

In this case, we can see a couple of problems with the teacher's thinking. First of all, the teacher has made an absolute moral claim by saying that Christians *should stop judging other people*. If there is no absolute standard of right and wrong, how can the teacher think that it is wrong to judge other people? Second, this type of thinking would be very difficult to live with. Almost everyone I know thinks that the Holocaust was a terrible crime—an evil, evil event. But if there is no right and wrong, the best we can say is that we didn't really like the Holocaust. That doesn't seem quite strong enough. The same goes for torturing babies or serial killing. Are they wrong? I think so, and I think most people will agree if you ask them.

But maybe your teacher is smart and knows that this is coming, so he or she says that it isn't really wrong, it just seems so in our culture (I've had people tell me this, to my amazement). At this point argument may be fruitless. So what do you do? Just leave. But as you're leaving, pick up the person's MP3 player and leave with it. Now, the person may get mad because you're stealing his or her MP3 player, but so what? After all, stealing isn't *wrong*, they just don't like it. Hopefully by now you see why moral relativism does not really hold up to close examination. (Of course, you shouldn't really steal your friend's stuff.) But simple people never get this far. They give up immediately and believe whatever is told them. Much better to give thought to your steps, and so to avoid potential embarrassment later when the thinking gets exposed as foolishness.

But What If... ?

The whole point of this chapter has been to assist you in making important decisions. When you need to make a decision, be sure to choose wisely! When instruction on the subject has been given, listen to what godly people have said—accept it as wise and beneficial. When faced with a decision that doesn't have instruction attached to it, seek advice from people you trust and who are qualified to give it. Above all, *think before you act!* Don't make a hasty decision.

Sometimes though, we make hasty decisions and realize it just a little too late. You may be asking yourself, "But what if I've already made a bad choice?" Proverbs has much to teach us in this regard too: "The prudent see danger and take refuge, but the simple keep going and suffer for it" (Proverbs 27:12). If you see danger in your future, hide yourself from it now. Only the foolish would keep going and suffer more as a result. If you have stopped working in school and started flunking your classes, start working again. Talk to your teachers about what is going on. If you are in a relationship that has turned sexual, get out of it. Stop having sex. Do not keep harming yourself just because you've made a bad choice. If you are doing drugs or drinking on the weekends without your parents knowing, get help before something serious happens. Do not be a fool. Turn around and get back on the right path. With God there is always forgiveness.

Memory Verse

"A simple man believes anything, but
a prudent man gives thought to his steps."
PROVERBS 14:15

Study Questions

1. What does it mean to accept instruction?

2. How does accepting instruction protect and honor us? How has it done this for you in your own life (or the life of someone you know)?

3. Do you consider yourself self-sufficient or not? How do you see this in your own life? Have you listened to advice from wise people or not?

4. Why might your friends not be the best source of advice? Why is it important to seek advice from the wise instead of the foolish?

5. What does making plans require? What can happen if we don't do this?

6. In what areas of your life do you feel you might have zeal without knowledge? What can you do to overcome this?

7. What should you do if you have made bad decisions?

FOUR

Those Pesky Parents

In the next five chapters, we will examine a series of relationships—relationships with parents, friends, the opposite sex, and God. I want to begin with one of the most important relationships you have at this stage of your life, your relationship with your parents. Now, teens and parents aren't famous for getting along very well. Most teens see their parents as hopelessly uncool, bent on ruining their fun, and always dispensing unwanted advice (you may call it "nagging"). No teen would seriously consider listening to this advice—I mean, who's going to take advice on what clothes to buy from someone who dresses like that?!

Still, most parents just want the best for their kids—that's why they give advice. In fact, a lot of Proverbs is a father giving advice to his son, as we saw earlier. He hopes his son will listen to the advice so that life can be as good as possible. Read what he says in Proverbs 4:1–4:

> Listen, my sons, to a father's instruction;
>   pay attention and gain understanding.
> I give you sound learning,
>   so do not forsake my teaching.
> When I was a boy in my father's house,
>   still tender, and an only child of my mother,
> he taught me and said,

"Lay hold of my words with all your heart;
keep my commands and you will live."

Here the father asks his son to listen to him because the advice he is giving is good. "If you listen to this advice—if you keep my commands—you will live." That is the whole point of the advice many parents give: to help you have the best possible life you can live. And remember, parents have been in this same boat before. This father knows the value of listening to parents because *he listened* to his father. Now he hopes his son will make the same wise choice.

The father repeats this idea a few chapters later, emphasizing the notion that his words will help bring the best in life.

My son, keep your father's commands
and do not forsake your mother's teaching.
Bind them upon your heart forever;
fasten them around your neck.
When you walk, they will guide you;
when you sleep, they will watch over you;
when you awake, they will speak to you.
For these commands are a lamp,
this teaching is a light,
and the corrections of discipline are the way to life,
keeping you from the immoral woman,
from the smooth tongue of the wayward wife.
PROVERBS 6:20–24

The father doesn't give these commands because he wants to ruin his son's chance of having any fun in life. Just the opposite: he wants to make sure his son will steer clear of some obvious pitfalls in life—the immoral woman, the wayward wife. He knows his advice will help guide and protect his son because his advice is wise, and that is what wisdom does for us.

Parents want the best for you, and that's why they give you so much advice. The amazing thing is *they may be right*. I know that's hard to swallow, but parents sometimes know what they're talking about. In fact, let's turn first to two proverbs that will remind us that our parents may be worth listening to.

Parents: Smarter than You Think

The shocking truth is that parents sometimes know what they are talking about. It turns out that your parents have lived a lot longer than you have, have had many more life experiences and have probably learned a lot along the way. You can learn a lot in school, but there are some things you just can't learn until you've lived them—or if you're wise enough to listen to someone who has already lived them. Parents can offer such wisdom because they have gone through life experiences that you're encountering for the first time—relational troubles, money problems, career decisions. Not every person who is older than you is wiser than you, but the chances improve. If you know some godly older men or women, they probably have lots of wisdom to offer you.

Proverbs says as much: "Gray hair is a crown of splendor; it is attained by a righteous life" (16:31). The point of this proverb is that God often blesses the righteous with a long life (not always—consider the disciples, all but one of whom died at a young age). But I love the idea of gray hair being a *crown of splendor*. In our image-conscious culture, we often do all that we can to avoid any traces of aging. Many people who have gray hair dye it so that no one can tell. But Proverbs takes a different spin on aging. It sees the signs of aging as a crown of splendor—as a sign of knowledge and wisdom gained along the way. Let me encourage you to look at your elders in the same light. Anytime you see your parents (or pastors, teachers, neighbors, etc.) as old—skin sagging, gray hair showing, clothes out of style—remember that each sign of aging is also proof of valuable life experiences—experiences that you haven't had as someone younger.

Let me give an example to show you how this might work. Suppose you come home one day with a new boyfriend or girlfriend. And let's also suppose that this guy or gal isn't exactly your parents' first choice, and for good reason (she's not a believer, he dropped out of high school to pursue a career in pyrotechnics—something like that). First of all, your parents *might* know what they are talking about. I have already seen several marriages collapse because young couples ignored the warnings of everyone around them and got married anyway—and your parents probably have too. So give them some credit right away.

But second, let's suppose you tell them, "You just don't understand. You don't know how we feel about each other." See, that's a silly statement. Your parents probably know exactly how you feel. They probably had feelings like yours at several points in their lives, and they now know through the wisdom they've accumulated across the years just how unreliable those feelings can be.

Gray hair means they've lived longer than you, and they deserve at least a second thought before blowing off their advice. Your parents, whether you want to admit it or not, are probably smarter than you think. Those older than us often have much to offer us in terms of life experience and wisdom. It will be far better for you to tap into that wisdom instead of assuming that—at the ripe old age of sixteen or eighteen or whatever—you already know everything you need to know in life.

Another proverb turns the traditional "teens vs. parents" mentality on its head. Proverbs 17:6 says, "Children's children are a crown to the aged, and parents are the pride of their children." I want to focus on the last part of this proverb—the idea that parents are the pride of their children. Let me ask you a simple question: are you proud of your parents? I suspect many would answer no. But why? I am sure with a little bit of thinking you could easily come up with ten or more reasons why you ought to take pride in your parents. I know how proud I am that my father served in the military during Vietnam, or how proud I am that my mom helped care for babies born addicted to cocaine. What about your parents? Can you think of any reason why you should be proud of them? I'm sure you can.

Taking pride in someone means giving them the respect they deserve. Think carefully about your parents now—all that they have done for you, the advice they've given that proved true in the end, their efforts to follow

God (if they are seeking him)—and see if they aren't worthy of some respect. If they are, give it to them. Show them that you take pride in them, thank them for what they have done for you, and listen to them when they speak. Remember, they've lived a lot longer than you, so they're probably smarter than you think!

I wish I didn't have to write this next part, but the fact of the matter is that too many children in this world have parents in whom they can take no pride. What respect does a parent deserve who abandons or abuses his or her kids? Remember that proverbs are *principles* not *promises*. That is, generally speaking, parents should be the pride of their children. But this does not always happen. If you have a parent who has *genuinely* treated you poorly (I'm not talking about a parent who doesn't let you go to Cancun with your friends for Spring Break; I'm talking about someone who has abused his children or left them altogether), I want to say two things to you. First, and perhaps most difficult, remember that God is your Father. And God is not like our earthly fathers and mothers—he is perfect, wholly loving towards you, and he will neither leave nor forsake you. Second, seek out parental figures—godly men and women who can help teach you what your parents did not. A teacher, pastor, neighbor, or friend can provide much of the same wisdom and advice that parents do. This can be a good idea for all of us. I had very good parents, thank God, but I still had a good friend, a teacher and member of my church, who helped me enormously during my formative teen years. Most parents will be grateful for the help they get in raising their teens!

We have talked now about making sure you honor your parents as older and wiser than you. Honor involves more than lip service, however. If you really want to honor your parents, you have to make sure you are living a life they can take pride in also. Remember, Proverbs 17:6 does not just say parents are the pride of their children; it also says children (and grandchildren) are a crown to the aged.

The Bane or Boon of Their Existence

Let's ask the simple question: are you a crown to your parents? Are your walk with God, your attitude, your relationships, your achievements jewels in the crown you have forged for them? Or is the crown you gave them more along the lines of those paper Burger King crowns you get with kids' meals? Proverbs reminds us that children can either be a parent's joy or grief—the bane or boon of their existence.

Proverbs 10:1 says, "A wise son brings joy to his father, but a foolish son grief to his mother." You have two choices here, as with so many other decisions we find in Proverbs: wisdom or foolishness. Choosing wisdom—choosing to listen to those older and wiser than you, choosing to follow God and his path for your life—will bring joy to your parents. As I said earlier, parents want the best for their children, and when their children do what is best, parents are happy. If your parents teach you the value of diligent study, they will rejoice when you come home with an 'A' on that really hard test you had to take.

Of course, the opposite is true too. Foolish children—those who scorn their parents' advice and God's wisdom for their lives—bring grief to everyone around them. Parents who have taught their children the value of integrity cringe when they discover their kids have been caught cheating. Parents who teach their children the importance of purity will weep when they learn their daughter is pregnant out of wedlock. Parents who have done their best to instill in their children a deep devotion to God will have their hearts broken by a son who leaves the faith. As a child, you have the opportunity by the choices you make to bring either joy or grief to your parents. Remember, "To have a fool for a son brings grief; there is no joy for the father of a fool" (Proverbs 17:21).

A similar proverb gives this discussion a slightly different nuance. Proverbs 15:20 teaches, "A wise son brings joy to his father, but a foolish man despises his mother." We have already looked at what the first part means: you can make your parents glad because of what you do. But note that in the second half of the proverb, this son doesn't bring his mother grief, he *despises* her. If you willfully cause your parents grief by ignoring their advice and making foolish choices, Proverbs makes it clear that you do it because you don't like them. Someone who cared about his or her parents would never make such a choice. This proverb draws out the pride and selfishness inherent in disobeying your parents. People like this think they have no need of anyone else's advice because they already know everything (pride) and so ignore the wishes and desires of those closest to them to pursue their own illicit desires (selfishness). Such people bring only grief to their parents because they despise those who love them most.

Discipline: For "Your" Good

In order to prevent children from causing them grief, parents must discipline their children—grounding them, taking away their cell phone or computer, withholding their allowance. Teenagers don't tend to like being disciplined. Really, nobody likes to be disciplined. We would much rather live lives free of consequences. But the fact is discipline is good for you. God gave you parents in part so they would discipline you, correct you, and help you from straying too far off course. Discipline is like a fence meant to keep toddlers inside the backyard. Sure, the toddler wishes he could get outside the fence to continue exploring, but that's because he doesn't know there's a lake nearby that he could drown in. The fence keeps him from drowning in the same way that discipline will keep you from really messing up your life.

In case you don't believe me that discipline is good for you, Proverbs says it's true. Proverbs 23:13–14 exhorts parents, "Do not withhold discipline from a child; / if you punish him with the rod, he will not die. / Punish him with the rod / and save his soul from death." According to this passage, parents *must discipline* their children in order to protect them. Effective discipline will keep the child on course such that his or her soul *will not die*—meaning the child can enjoy an eternity in the presence of God in heaven. Children who lead undisciplined lives—living lives free of consequences—will face the consequences eventually. We should be grateful for the discipline we receive on earth because it will spare us "discipline" for eternity. As Proverbs 19:18 says, "Discipline your son, for in that there is hope; do not be a willing party to his death." No parents want willingly to consign their children to hell, and discipline is one way in which they can help avoid that fate.

Discipline will prepare your soul for eternity, but it has an immediate benefit too. Several proverbs demonstrate the value of discipline in the here and now. First, Proverbs 22:15 notes, "Folly is bound up in the heart of a child, but the rod of discipline will drive it far from him." We are all born fools (theologians call this original sin), but discipline, coupled with God's work in our lives, can help us overcome this foolishness. We shouldn't want to be fools, because fools face all sorts of disastrous consequences in their lives. Discipline will help prevent this. Suppose as a child you have a tendency to lie a lot. Hopefully your parents will discipline you each time you lie to them to help break you of the habit. You have faced the consequences as a young child who lied about eating some cookies before dinner. That's not too bad. Imagine now that your parents never disciplined you. How is your spouse going to respond to your constant lying? What about your boss? Your friends? You will be single, unemployed, and lonely before you know it. Discipline could have driven this folly from your heart—after all, it's for your own good.

Likewise, Proverbs 22:6—one of the best known proverbs—teaches, "Train a child in the way he should go, and when he is old he will not turn from it." Training involves discipline, as any athletic coach knows. If you want to become a successful soccer player, you've got to learn to kick the ball correctly. And if you're not kicking it right, your coach will correct you—which is precisely what discipline is. In the same way, your parents will correct you—your morals, values, attitude, actions—so that you can play this "game" of life better. If you respond to your training well, you'll be better equipped for life. Proverbs says you will not turn from this training later on. Returning to our earlier example, once your parents have trained you not to lie, you should remain truthful throughout your life.

Discipline is one of the most unwelcome acts in most people's lives. At the same time, we should see discipline as a tremendous gift to us. God places people in our lives to discipline, correct, and train us so that we can grow and learn from our mistakes. This brings me to my next point—how we should respond to discipline.

Discipline: "The Glad Surrender"

The great Christian writer Elisabeth Elliot calls discipline "the glad surrender," meaning a lifestyle of joyful obedience, dependence, and responsibility.[1] If discipline really is good for you, as I argued above, then one ought to respond to it with glad surrender, letting whatever correction needs to happen take place in your life. Many proverbs teach the wisdom of submitting to discipline because discipline is good for us.

Proverbs 15:32 says, "He who ignores discipline despises himself, but whoever heeds correction gains understanding." I find this proverb very interesting. The second part—that "whoever heeds correction gains understanding"—seems simple enough. Listening to correction will always lead to an increase in understanding, just like listening to a coach will help improve your play. It is the first part that catches my eye: "He who ignores discipline *despises himself*." People who reject correction and discipline do so at great risk to themselves. They may think they're getting away with whatever they want by sneaking out when grounded or skipping a detention, but in reality they are simply passing up an opportunity to learn from their mistakes. And people who don't learn from their mistakes keep on making them. These people ruin their lives—despise themselves—because they refuse to surrender to discipline.

Once again, we're faced with a choice: do we accept or reject discipline? Do we act wisely or foolishly? Proverbs 15:5 lays out the choice for us: "A fool spurns his father's discipline, but whoever heeds correction shows prudence." Fools—those who despise themselves—ignore all the advice their parents give them, all the discipline and correction they should have received. On the other hand, those who listen to their parents' advice, who heed correction, show themselves to be wise. As someone who disciples a lot of high school students, I've seen many teenagers have to make this choice. When I sit someone down to have a hard talk with them—about drinking, relationships with the opposite sex, dressing modestly—I can separate the wise from the foolish in the first few seconds or so. Some listen to what I have to say or what their parents and youth pastors have said, and they make good choices and grow in their faith; others make excuses, ignore the advice they're given and, well, you know the rest.

It is so sad to see some choose poorly, because they have the opportunity to grow right before them, but they reject it. Proverbs 12:1 gets at the heart of the matter when it says, "Whoever loves discipline loves knowledge, but he who hates correction is stupid." Some kids want to grow wiser, so they listen to people disciplining them. Others show themselves to be stupid (foolish) by letting such a great opportunity pass them by. No wonder Proverbs 25:12 says, "Like an earring of gold or an ornament of fine gold is a wise man's rebuke to a listening ear." Ears that listen to correction and rebuke ought to have special ornamentation in them, so everyone knows that these ears belong to someone who loves wisdom. See how surprised your parents are when you tell them you want to get this kind of jewelry in your ear instead of getting a piercing in your lip or eyebrow or wherever else people are punching holes in themselves now!

What Happens If I Don't?

I have suggested a number of times in this chapter that respecting your parents and listening to what they say will do you a lot more good than harm. But it gets more serious than that. In two strong passages, Proverbs describes the consequences of ignoring your parents, of living a life of willful folly and disobedience. Proverbs 11:29 says, "He who brings trouble on his family will inherit only wind, and the fool will be servant to the wise." Imagine a group of children gathered around their father's deathbed, awaiting his blessing and his last will and testament. He moves from one sibling to the next, leaving property, money, prized possessions, until at last he comes to you. Now, you've been the black sheep of the family, the prodigal son or daughter who never returned. What can you expect to inherit? How about nothing? This proverb says you expect to inherit the wind, a Hebrew metaphor for zip, zilch, nada, and nothing.

People who trouble their family cut ties with those closest to them who can best help them in times of need. As a result, when trouble comes, they have no one to turn to. Remember, proverbs are principles, not promises, so it may be that someone will have gracious parents who will still take care of them—but are you willing to take that chance? This proverb also teaches that this type of foolishness has lifelong consequences. If you don't accept instruction, if you don't try to bring your parents joy and honor, you'll probably end up working for someone who did. It is simple really. One kid listens to his parents when they teach him the importance of study, works hard in school, and when he graduates, gets a good job. What about the other kid, the one who ignored his parents and spent his time drinking instead of doing homework? Proverbs says he'll be working for the kid who listened to Mom and Dad.

Proverbs 30:17 makes the same point, only much more dramatically. It says, "The eye that mocks a father, / that scorns obedience to a mother, / will be pecked out by the ravens of the valley, / will be eaten by the vultures." Not a pretty picture, but certainly a vivid one. What is this proverb teaching? This proverb pictures a proud son or daughter, represented by their haughty eye, looking down on his or her parents. Interestingly, the Hebrew for this proverb actually reads "that looks down on the *gray hair* of a mother."[2] As we saw earlier, gray hair represents the wealth of wisdom accumulated through age and experience. Foolish children sneer at their parents' age instead of honoring it. The eye that looks down on parents in this way meets an ignominious end—plucked out by a raven, and then devoured by a vulture. This image pictures the dead body in a desert devoid of any other food, a feast for a gathering of birds. Most children, should they die before their parents, would expect a proper burial. But this child looked down on his parents, scorned their advice, and met a tragic, tragic end. I hope you will choose better.

Conclusion

In concluding this important chapter dealing with perhaps your most important earthly relationship at this stage of your life, I want only to quote a short passage that summarizes all the teaching we've gleaned so far on this topic from Proverbs.

> Listen to your father, who gave you life,
>   and do not despise your mother when she is old.
> Buy the truth and do not sell it;
>   get wisdom, discipline and understanding.

The father of a righteous man has great joy;
he who has a wise son delights in him.
May your father and mother be glad;
may she who gave you birth rejoice!
PROVERBS 23:22–25

MEMORY VERSE

"A wise son brings joy to his father, but a foolish son grief to his mother."
PROVERBS 10:1

Study Questions

1. Why do you think your parents give you so much advice?

2. What makes your parents worth listening to? Can you think of any examples of times when they were right in the advice they gave you?

3. Do you think of gray hair as a "crown of splendor" or a fashion blunder? Why?

4. What are some reasons you are proud of your parents?

5. Do you think you are a crown to your parents? Why or why not? Would you like to be? How will you become one?

6. How is rebelling against your parents the same as despising them?

7. How is discipline good for us? When have you been disciplined and discovered that it had been good for you?

8. How is ignoring discipline the same as despising yourself?

FIVE

Real Friendship

Establishing a good relationship with your parents will prove to be one of the wisest decisions you will ever make. In the same way, carefully choosing friends—establishing relationships with the right kind of people—will have a lasting impact on your life. Proverbs offers us a number of important insights on both how to choose friends and how to be a good friend. Let's turn first to how to choose friends wisely.

Choosing Friends

Choosing friends wisely can be a difficult task. We are often most concerned with choosing friends whose interests and hobbies mirror our own rather than examining the possible benefit or harm that friendship might cause us. Proverbs 13:20 sets the standard for us: "He who walks with the wise grows wise, but a companion of fools suffers harm." Simple, isn't it? If you hang around with wise people (and remember, in Proverbs "wise" refers to our actions too!), you'll grow wiser. If you hang around with foolish people, you'll get hurt.

When you spend time with people, you become like them. You will start to talk like them, act like them, dress like them. In fact, they have a saying in Colombia, where I live: "Tell me who your friends are, and I'll tell you who you will become." Colombians are so convinced of the connection between one's friends and one's behavior that they think they can predict who you'll become simply by knowing your friends! And I think they're right. Walk with the wise, get wise; walk with the foolish, get hurt.

It is not hard to understand how this works. Our environment influences us tremendously. If you play in the mud, you are bound to get muddy. It is just that simple. Same with your friends: if you've got "muddy" friends, you are going to get dirty eventually. Test it out if you don't believe me. Watch what happens if you start hanging around with someone who swears a lot. See if you don't start having swear words pop into your head when they never used to. I can't tell you the number of people I've known who left for college promising me they wouldn't start drinking. But then they started hanging out with people who drink (it's not too hard to find those kinds of people in college), and within *weeks* they were drinking! Now I am not talking here about whether drinking is a sin or not. I am simply saying that these people—who had promised not to start drinking—did so as soon as they chose friends who did.

Proverbs promises us that we will become like our friends. In Proverbs 22:24–25, it says, "Do not make friends with a hot-tempered man, / do not associate with one easily angered, / or you may learn his ways / and get yourself ensnared." If you choose a friend who is a hothead, always getting into fights with everybody—parents, teachers, other friends—you will eventually develop a temper yourself. You will *learn his ways*, and that has consequences. The phrase "and get yourself ensnared" actually says "and fetch yourself a snare."[1] Snares are used in hunting to trap animals. So why would anyone want to fetch a snare for himself? It doesn't make any sense. But that's exactly what people do when they choose foolish friends. They are setting traps for themselves, and eventually they are going to get hurt.

Hot-tempered friends aren't the only ones who will get you into trouble. Proverbs 23:20–21 tells us, "Do not join those who drink too much wine / or gorge themselves on meat, / for drunkards and gluttons become poor, / and drowsiness clothes them in rags." The problem with people who eat too much or who get drunk is that they will eventually become poor. I have known a few people in my life who have been fired because of their drinking habits. But that's beside the point for now. The question is why shouldn't we make friends with drunkards and gluttons? Sure, they'll become poor, but what does that matter to us? Well, Proverbs seems to hint that we'll end up the same way. You have to connect the dots, but once you do, the picture becomes clear. If you hang around with people who drink too much, you're liable to start drinking too much, and then you're going to end up in poverty too.

Or consider Proverbs 24:1–2: "Do not envy wicked men, / do not desire their company; / for their hearts plot violence, / and their lips talk about making trouble." What's the trouble with wicked men? They plot violence and cause trouble. Easy enough. But what's the trouble with desiring their company? Most likely, we will become like them. And that means that we will plot violence and cause trouble, both of which have consequences. Don't be a fool—don't ensnare yourself!

When choosing friends, be sure that you choose friends who will not hurt you spiritually. We can have a "good time" with all sorts of people, but only some of those people will help us to better ourselves. Those are the people we should befriend. The others will be of no help to us, and more likely, they will hurt us. My advice to you is that of Proverbs 14:7: "Stay away from a foolish man, for you will not find knowledge on his lips." Seek friends on whose lips you will find knowledge. In other words, seek friends who will help you to grow spiritually. Walk with the wise, get wise; walk with the foolish, get hurt.

Being a Good Friend

Choosing friends is important, but so is being a good friend. That is, you want to make sure *you* are the type of person who will help others, not hurt them. Proverbs gives us some excellent advice on how to be a good friend. We will look at three areas in particular: loyalty, confrontation, and boundaries.

Loyalty

A true friend—the kind of friend you want to be—is a loyal friend. Loyalty means standing by your friend no matter what—hard times, interpersonal conflicts, or whatever. Many teenagers do not prove to be very loyal friends. I work in a high school, and I see how often friends turn against each other because of petty differences—a bit of gossip, liking the same boy or girl, a misinterpreted facial expression, or something else equally meaningless. But this is not the standard of Scripture. This is not what it means to be a good friend.

Proverbs 17:17 says, "A friend loves at all times, and a brother is born for adversity." A friend—a true friend—loves *at all times*. That is loyalty. This friend does not abandon you because you are suffering, but sticks by you. This friend *loves* you. And what does it mean for a friend to love? I think of the words of Paul the apostle in First Corinthians 13:4–7: "Love is patient, love is kind. It does not envy, it does not boast, it is not proud. It is not rude, it is not self-seeking, it is not easily angered, it keeps no record of wrongs. Love does not delight in evil but rejoices with the truth. It always protects, always trusts, always hopes, always perseveres." A true friend loves in this way. We should not look to our own interests, but to those of our friends; we should not keep a tally of all the ways our friends have hurt us (and believe me, friends hurt each other!), but practice forgiveness and humility; not believing the worst about people, but always believing—hoping for—the best. A loyal friend loves at all times.

How different this friendship is than that based on circumstances! Circumstances change, but we should not abandon our friends as a result. Some people only stick by their friends when things are going well. "Wealth brings many friends, but a poor man's friend deserts him," says Proverbs 19:4. But what type of friends are we talking about? Many people who befriend the rich do so only to see what they can get from them. But that is self-seeking, so it cannot be love, so it cannot be true friendship. And others abandon the poor because the poor can't give them anything at all. But this is not friendship in any meaningful sense of the word.

True friendship requires loyalty. "A man of many companions may come to ruin, but there is a friend who sticks closer than a brother" (Proverbs 18:24). We see in this proverb two classes of "friends": the companion-type, who only wants to know what the friend can do for him, and the brother-type, who sticks close no matter what. Which friend will you be? Will you desert your friends when they are no longer popular, when they no longer have anything to offer you? Or will you be faithful to them the way God has stayed faithful to you? The choice is yours.

So how will you choose? Loyal friend or not? Companion or brother? How will you choose when you discover that your best friend likes the same boy you do? Will you abandon the friendship in pursuit of some flimsy notion of romantic love (we'll get to that in the next chapter)? Or will you recognize that *probably* you are not going to meet your husband (or wife) in high school, and that the friendship should be more important? Will you draw daggers and fight to the death for Mr. Perfect? Or will you humbly stick by your friend, wishing the best for her? The choice is yours.

How will you choose when many in your circle of acquaintances turn against a friend of yours because he has chosen to stand for truth? Will you stand with him and risk being mocked yourself? Or will you cowardly watch as he endures the ridicule of his former friends? I can remember as a sophomore in high school taking a stand for abstinence in my health class. The whole class laughed at me, which really didn't bother me much. What bothered me was knowing that I had Christian friends in that class who wouldn't stand with me. Will you do better than my friends did? The choice is yours.

Confrontation

Some may be confused now, as confrontation and loyalty seem at odds with one another. If you're loyal to a friend, how can you rebuke her? But let me assure you, confrontation is as much a part of being a true friend as loyalty is. Proverbs 27:5 says, "Better is open rebuke than hidden love." This proverb can be difficult to understand at first glance. What comparison is actually being made? The question is which one actually benefits the friend. Hidden love does nothing to help the loved one. Writing love notes and then tearing them up does not reveal my affection for someone. Only by actually showing the person that I love her will it matter. I have to give the love note to the girl of my dreams in order for her to know that I love her. But that is precisely how open rebuke functions: it is a "love note," letting a friend know that you care for them.

Think about it: confrontation is an ugly affair. It takes a tremendous amount of courage; feelings can get hurt, the person may get defensive and lash out at you. Given how much is at risk, you would really have to care about someone in order to confront him. You would have to care more about his well-being than you do about your comfort level. So open rebuke is open love. And it is so much better than hidden love because it actually benefits your friend.

I suspect this is why Proverbs teaches, "Wounds from a friend can be trusted, but an enemy multiplies kisses" (27:6). During godly confrontation, a friend may have to wound another. But these wounds are like the wounds of a surgeon's scalpel: they bring life and healing even as they sting. And so, true friends can trust the pain they may have to cause each other. Ironically, it is the enemy who makes the grandest show of love, multiplying kisses. Oftentimes we are happier pretending we see nothing amiss in our friend's life, and so do nothing to help. To the world, this seems like friendship, like tolerance—overlooking another's faults and persisting in friendship. But in the end, this is the work of an enemy because it cares more for the preservation of a superficial comfort within the friendship than it does for the person's deepest spiritual needs. Such "friends" would rather avoid a painful conversation than stop their friends from destroying themselves. We must confront our friends to help them grow.

How does confrontation help our friends grow? (And how can it help us grow?) Basically, godly confrontation helps us to see areas where we struggle, giving us the opportunity to change for the better. Proverbs uses the analogy of a sword being sharpened to make this point: "As iron sharpens iron, so one man sharpens another" (27:17). Confrontation sharpens us, helps us to be more effective instruments for God's service. We all, I hope, want to grow in Christlikeness. Without confrontation we will never get there. We need our friends to help us grow, and we need to be the type of friends who will help others to grow.

A word of caution here: confrontation is not license for being an arrogant jerk. The point is not to get to tell everybody how stupid or foolish they are to make yourself feel better. That's not godly at all. The point is *lovingly* and *sensitively* to help your friend grow in godliness. You need to make sure your attitude, your words, your tone of voice, all reflect this goal. Do not confront people in front of others. That will only make them feel small and stupid; it will not help them grow. Take them off to the side and let them know that you have their best interests in mind. And then, in a gentle voice, tell them what you noticed. Give them time to explain—you may have misunderstood what they said or did. If that's the case, apologize for having been wrong. Remember, when confronting someone, there may be sparks (that's what happens when iron hits iron), but you can do a lot to keep the sparks from burning anyone.

So when do you confront a friend? I can think of two main areas of confrontation. The first is very easy. You need to confront a Christian friend when she is blatantly sinning against God. Regrettably, I had to do this with a good friend of mine in high school who had begun having quite a bit of sex on prom night. She had been interviewed by the school newspaper a few weeks before, and had taken a very public stand for Christ. Now the whole school knew she had been engaging in promiscuous sex. For the sake of her soul *and for the Christian witness* at my school, I needed to confront her. You may have to confront friends who are likewise caught up in sexual immorality, lying to parents, cheating, or the like.

The second is a bit trickier. You need to confront a Christian friend who has offended someone in a personal relationship. This is trickier because it is very rarely a black-and-white issue, the way most sin issues are. So in this case in particular, you need to have a humble attitude when confronting the friend. You may even want to begin with some questions to make sure you understand the issue. But if you were right, you can let the person know what he did wrong and how he can do it better. As Christians, we are called to love our neighbors—with our speech and actions—and I know that I often need the insights of my wife and friends to see how I have failed here. So you may have to confront friends who have been careless in their speech (gossiping or making fun of someone, being very sharp in their speech) or actions (blowing off a friend because a better invitation came around, being loyal).

I should add a word here before looking at the last section. In many ways, being a loyal friend and a friend who confronts when needed simply means being a Christlike friend. Jesus showed us the way in this area as in so many. Though his friends deserted him—especially as he was being arrested in the Garden of Gethsemane—he remained faithful to them. Just remember, he stood on trial, waiting to be executed as a criminal for the sins of fallen humanity *even as his best friend denied even knowing him three times!* That is true loyalty. And Christ was willing to confront his friends. Most famously, Christ rebuked Peter—calling him Satan (which I wouldn't recommend for you when you confront your friends)—when Peter looked for an earthly rather than a heavenly kingdom (see Mark 8:31-33). Of course, Peter learned from this and other confrontations and became a pillar in the church. We, as Christians, are called to be like Christ, and that includes in our friendships.

Boundaries

I will say only a few words about the last area. As true friends, we need to be careful of the boundaries that ought to exist between friends. Proverbs does not say much about this issue, but one passage does offer some insight into the issue. "If you find honey, eat just enough— / too much of it, and you will vomit. / Seldom set foot in your neighbor's house— / too much of you, and he will hate you" (Proverbs 25:16-17). This passage has an implied comparison. Eating honey is just like hanging out at a friend's house. Too much of either and somebody's liable to get sick. If you eat too much honey (or ice cream, as the case may be), you'll probably have a stomachache. Likewise, if you keep showing up at somebody's house, she'll probably get sick of you.

I wouldn't have even mentioned this issue since only one proverb really pertains to it, except that I have known so many teenagers who desperately needed this bit of advice. It is great to have friends, and it is great to be with your friends. But be careful, because you don't want to lose your friends. Asking them to hang out *all* of the time, showing up *all* of the time, always being around—these can all make someone get real sick of you real fast. Make sure you are being sensitive to the other person's schedule, other responsibilities, other friends. Too much of you, and, well, he'll probably hate you.

MEMORY VERSE

"He who walks with the wise grows wise, but a companion of fools suffers harm."
PROVERBS 13:20

Study Questions

1. Why is it so important to choose friends wisely? Do you think the Colombian "proverb" is true? Why or why not?

2. What will happen if you start hanging out with the wrong types of people? Can you think of any examples from your own life when this has happened?

3. What kind of friend do you want to be? How will you become that type of friend?

4. Are you a companion-type or a brother-type of friend? What circumstances have affected your friendships?

5. What makes confronting a friend so difficult? What makes it worthwhile?

6. What boundaries could you keep with your friends?

SIX

SEX EDUCATION

While the chances of you meeting the person with whom you will spend the rest of your life are slim in high school, the possibility of wrecking that relationship before it begins is very real—even at a young age. In its comments on sex, Proverbs offers us some invaluable wisdom on how to overcome that terrifying prospect—and how to establish patterns of behavior that will help you to cherish the relationship once it comes. While Proverbs offers mostly negative advice—how to avoid pitfalls in this area—I want to begin with the positive.

IDEAL LOVE

Proverbs offers us a beautiful picture of marriage, of the ideal love between a man and woman. Listen to the words of Proverbs 5:15–19:

> Drink water from your own cistern,
> running water from your own well.
> Should your springs overflow in the streets,
> your streams of water in the public squares?
> Let them be yours alone, never to be shared with strangers.
> May your fountain be blessed,
> and may you rejoice in the wife of your youth.

A loving doe, a graceful deer—
and may her breasts satisfy you always, may you ever be
captivated by her love.

This is how love was meant to be: absolute sexual fidelity and total marital bliss. Although you're probably not married yet, it's good to take a look at the type of marriage you want to have—to plan for the future you desire.

Sexual Fidelity

Proverbs plays on the imagery of a well in describing how marriage ought to be. This is not surprising, as the image of drinking is often used to suggest sexual pleasure. Consider Proverbs 9:17, where it says "Stolen water is sweet," obviously a reference to adultery. Similarly, in Song of Songs 4:15, the man says to his beloved, "You are a garden fountain, a well of flowing water streaming down from Lebanon." Michael Fox, commenting on Proverbs 5:15-19, says, "The image suggests cool, limpid refreshment for hot desires, which are slaked by 'drinking,' that is, lovemaking."[1] The whole key is *what* you drink to satisfy those desires.

As a faithful husband, you need to drink from your well only. This section of Proverbs is addressed to a son, so the father figure compares the son's wife to the well. If you already have a well, why would you need to steal water from someone else's? That doesn't make any sense. In the same way, if you already have a loving wife, why would you seek comfort in the embrace of another? Drink water from your own well. That is the husband's duty: to remain absolutely faithful sexually.

But the wife has the same duty. Still using the metaphor of the well, the writer asks, "Should your springs overflow in the streets, your streams of water in the public squares?" A husband shouldn't steal water from someone else's well, but it doesn't make any sense for his well to become the community well either. A wife should provide "water" for her husband only. Proverbs says as much: "Let them [the waters] be yours alone, never to be shared with strangers." Absolute sexual fidelity—by both the husband and the wife—serves as the foundation for the marital bliss that Proverbs describes.

Marital Bliss

Being faithful in marriage will lead to greater happiness. And finding great joy in marriage will spur you on to faithfulness. The two work together. So after setting absolute sexual fidelity as the standard, the father makes some wishes for his son: "May your fountain be blessed, and may you rejoice in the wife of your youth." The first part continues the metaphor of a well or fountain, and here suggests the idea of the womb. In blessing the "fountain," the father is asking God to bless the couple with many children. But the second blessing is the one I want to look at carefully now.

"May you rejoice in the wife of your youth." It seems so simple, and yet it is so profound. The key to marital happiness is to *delight* in one another. Love can grow cold if you let it. But how much better to fan continuously the flames of love! To ensure that his son do as much, the father reminds him what a catch she is: "a loving doe, a graceful deer." Now, I know we don't tend to think of deer as being the sexiest animal on the planet, but the Hebrews often used the image of a deer to suggest beauty, grace, and yes, even sexiness. In Song of Songs, for example, the man compares his lover's breasts to "two fawns, like twin fawns of a gazelle that browse among the lilies" (4:5). This gets even more intense. The word "loving," in "loving doe," refers to the act of *lovemaking*. It seems clear that these two people are very much in love, but this part here refers *just* to the sexual aspect. Ideal love means an ideal sex life—you can't have one without the other.

The father figure continues with two more blessings: "May her breasts satisfy you always, may you ever be captivated by her love." That he singles out breasts as the part that will satisfy always suggests that he's still thinking of sexual love. In fact, some scholars even think that we should translate the word "breasts" as "lovemaking." This is steamy stuff. And the word for "satisfy" again brings up the image of drinking. We could almost translate this verse as "quench your thirst with her lovemaking."

The last blessing—to be ever captivated by her love—gets at the idea of "getting lost" in erotic pleasure. The sexual union of a man and his wife proves an unfathomable mystery, and one that every married couple should explore—getting lost in the search. Proverbs 30:18–19 says,

There are three things that are too amazing for me,
four that I do not understand:
the way of an eagle in the sky,
the way of a snake on a rock,
the way of a ship on the high seas,
and *the way of a man with a maiden*. (Emphasis added)

The way of a man with a maiden is an amazing thing. And once you're married, Proverbs tells us to plumb the depths of this mystery with energy and enthusiasm!

Does It Work?

Before we continue, I want to pause here and ask a simple question: does it work? Does the teaching of Proverbs actually work in real life, or should I believe what *Cosmopolitan* and MTV tell me? It's a fair question, one we desperately need to answer. After all, the Bible was written a long time ago—by people who had a very Victorian view of sex (which I'm not sure is true at all, but that's beside the point)—so maybe it's a tad outdated.

Well, I've done the research, and it turns out the Bible is right (surprise, surprise). Study after study confirms what Christians have known for years: devoted married couples have the best sex lives. This flies in the face of everything we hear from our culture. Television shows like *Sex in the City* and *Desperate Housewives*, just about every "romantic" comedy ever made, and every magazine in the supermarket check-out line tell us that singles have more fun. Maybe you should even postpone marriage for a bit to make sure you get your fun in before settling down into the doldrums of married life. But this simply is not true!

Take a look at these facts. Married women have more orgasms than single women (not at all surprising since a woman needs to feel completely safe to have an orgasm). A University of Chicago survey discovered that sexually faithful married couples report the highest sexual satisfaction, while singles and sexually unfaithful marrieds have the lowest.[2] And even more interestingly, strongly religious women report the best sex lives of all—rated both subjectively (how they feel about their sex lives) and objectively (frequency of orgasm).

The plain fact of the matter is that sex the way God intended it is always going to be the best sex—really, the only good sex. Why? Because sex is more than a physical act. It is the union of physical, intellectual, emotional, and spiritual intimacy, and that is why it is such a precious act. The sex that the world offers us only brings the physical, and that will *never* be as satisfying as the love God intends for you. I wish I could make you feel the frustration I have seen on the faces and hearts of some people very close to me who engaged in promiscuous sex—they are not happy anymore. I know of one married man—married for only a year!—who told me that he doesn't care about sex anymore because he had it so much before he got married. He would rather his wife let him watch a football game in peace and quiet than that she have sex with him. How sad. How much less than all that God wants us to enjoy.

So the next time you come across a *Cosmopolitan* headline that tells you how great sex before marriage is (as I did yesterday in the supermarket check-out line), remember, you've got truth on your side. Sex God's way will always be the best way—and you will enjoy (!) the benefits for the rest of your life.

Warnings against Sexual Immorality

As I said, I wanted to begin with the positive—with a picture of all that God intends sex to be in our lives. But Proverbs offers us a number of very stern warnings about what can happen when we let that ecstasy slip from our view.

Just before Proverbs paints the picture of ideal love, it offers this warning:

> For the lips of an adulteress drip honey,
> and her speech is smoother than oil;
> but in the end she is bitter as gall,
> sharp as a double-edged sword.
> Her feet go down to death;
> her steps lead straight to the grave. (5:3–5)

Here we see the hollow promise of sexual immorality. Although the lips of an adulteress drip honey—considered to be *the* dessert of choice in the Hebrew mind—she ends up tasting like a tall, refreshing glass of vinegar. Although her promises of pleasure pour forth like oil, in the end, they lead only to death and destruction—swords are in her mouth. Follow after her, and you'll have a very short walk into the grave.

Sexual immorality makes all the same promises as the adulteress. It promises pleasure, joy, fulfillment—but it can offer none of these. These promises are as empty as treaties broken before they are signed. As we saw above, sexual immorality will not provide sexual pleasure in the same way that sex within marriage will. But it can offer significantly greater harm. Some consequences are obvious—sexually transmitted diseases, unintended pregnancy, and the like. But some are much less obvious, and in many ways more damaging—feeling used and exploited, desensitization to God's gift of sexual pleasure, an inability to trust anyone completely.

Proverbs presents this descent into hell in dramatic fashion. Read chapter 7 now. The first twenty verses describe the seduction. We have already seen how this progresses—the hollow promises of 5:3–5. As 7:21 says, "With persuasive words she led him astray; she seduced him with her smooth talk." But now comes the descent.

All at once he followed her
 like an ox going to the slaughter,
like a deer stepping into a noose
 till an arrow pierces his liver,
like a bird darting into a snare,
 little knowing it will cost him his life.
Now then, my sons, listen to me;
 pay attention to what I say.
Do not let your heart turn to her ways
 or stray into her paths.
Many are the victims she has brought down;
 her slain are a mighty throng.

Her house is a highway to the grave,
leading down to the chambers of death.
PROVERBS 7:22–27

Such is the inevitable consequence of sexual immorality. One little knows how severe the ramifications will be until it is too late. A deer does not realize what trouble it is in until the arrow pierces it; a bird cannot see the end when it first gets caught in the snare. Neither do most people see the destruction they wreak upon their lives when they give in to sexual temptation.

At first, sexual temptation seems a road paved with gold—almost endless pleasure available to any who would walk it. But in fact, it is a "highway to the grave, leading down to the chambers of death." Would you walk down a road if you saw a pile of dead bodies at the end of it? Probably not. So why would you ever consider walking down this road? "Many are the victims she has brought down; her slain are a mighty throng."

Avoiding Temptation

So now that we know we need to avoid temptation, the question arises, how? How do we ensure that we won't get on the "highway to the grave," especially considering how many cultural influences push us in that direction? Fortunately, Proverbs offers us some advice about this issue too, two ways that we can avoid sexual immorality.

First, make sure you have a sober, rational outlook on the matter. "Do not lust in your heart after her beauty / or let her captivate you with her eyes, / for the prostitute reduces you to a loaf of bread, / and the adulteress preys upon your very life" (Proverbs 6:25–26). That guy or girl across the room may be absolutely gorgeous, but don't let that keep you from thinking. Use your head! You know that these people see you as a piece of meat—a "loaf of bread," according to Proverbs, but the idea is the same: they see you not as a person created in the image of God, but as a means to satisfy some minor physical cravings. Why would you give in to someone like that? Give them a candy bar and tell them to shove off. After all, they "prey upon your very life." They will destroy you if you let them. So don't.

Second, don't play around with this area; it's far too dangerous. "Can a man scoop fire into his lap without his clothes being burned? Can a man walk on hot coals without his feet being scorched?" (Proverbs 6:27–28). I think this is one of the most important proverbs for teenagers. Too often I see young adults scooping fire into their laps, thinking that the laws of science don't apply to them. Well, I've got news for you: unless you've coated your pants with asbestos, you're going to get burned. I have seen kids drinking all weekend long, never thinking that they might make a bad choice, get behind the wheel of a car and kill someone, or get caught—by their parents or worse. But we're talking about sex here, not drinking.

So what would it mean to scoop fire into your lap sexually? You probably don't need my help here. A bit of common sense should do it. Do you think lying next to your boyfriend or girlfriend on the couch, late at night, with no lights on, and a steamy movie on TV involves scooping fire into your lap? Yeah, probably. Lying next to your boyfriend or girlfriend just about anywhere can be bad enough, especially if "next to" really means "sort of on top of." What about having your boyfriend or girlfriend come over some time when your parents aren't home, when nobody's home but you two lovebirds? Yeah, probably. This doesn't just apply to couples, mind you. A girl or guy coming up to you, telling you how good you look, asking you to dance—that can be scooping fire into your lap, too. I know of a high school student who ended up making a very bad choice in just that situation. She'd been bamboozled by the "you're so beautiful line." (Which takes us back to bit of advice number one—remember, he thinks you're just a piece of meat!)

The bottom line is, play with matches and you're bound to get burned. So if you want to avoid that unpleasant fate (and I hope, looking at how great sex can be within marriage, you do want to avoid it), the advice is simple: don't play with matches. Don't mess around with something so important to God—and something that should be so important to you too.

Memory Verse

"Can a man scoop fire into his lap without his clothes being burned?"
Proverbs 6:27

Study Questions

1. How can a person ruin a marriage before it starts?

2. What type of marriage do you desire? What will you do to achieve it?

3. How is sex important to the marriage relationship?

4. Are the statistics on sex surprising to you? Why or why not? What makes God's way better?

5. What are some of the disastrous consequences of sexual immorality?

6. What are some ways to avoid temptation? What practical steps can you take to do this in your own life?

SEVEN

The Woman of Excellence

with Amy Cooper

Scripture rarely speaks to only one gender, and when it does, that gender is often male. On those rare occasions where the Bible does speak specifically to women, it is well worth our time to pay careful attention to what it is saying. Fortunately, Proverbs has a wealth of material directed specifically at women. Girls, you'll want to study these proverbs carefully to learn how best to be the woman God crafted you to be. Boys, you'll want to study these too, but for different reasons. As men, we will have to relate to women everyday, and so it will be useful to learn what you might look for in a future wife, or how to raise daughters, should the Lord bless you with them. I hope you all will pay these verses as close a reading as you pay all the others studied in this book.

It is worth issuing a warning here. Gender is a hot topic in the world today. Many do not want to talk about these types of issues for fear of being politically incorrect. In fact, many have gone so far as to deny any differences—emotional, psychological, even physical!—between the sexes. Thus, even to whisper many of the insights Proverbs teaches on this subject will invite a harsh response—sometimes even by other Christians. I ask only that you give these verses a fair and careful reading, and then submit yourselves to the teaching of the Scriptures. There are few dangers as great as making Scripture agree with us, rather than vice versa. In order to ensure I write from a balanced perspective, I have co-written this chapter with my wife, Amy. So rest assured this will not be one male's perspective, but one couple's attempt to understand the Bible on this difficult point.

What Type of Wife?

To begin, we have to understand that in speaking to women, Proverbs speaks to wives and mothers. As this is a book aimed at young adults, I'll assume very few of you are in these roles already. Still, the majority of you will get married and have children someday, and it is worth preparing for those roles wherever you are in life. One question Proverbs asks implicitly is what type of wife will you be? Specifically—and repeatedly—Proverbs warns against becoming a quarrelsome wife. Take, for example, Proverbs 21:9 and 21:19: "Better to live on a corner of the roof than share a house with a quarrelsome wife," and "Better to live in a desert than with a quarrelsome and ill-tempered wife." These two proverbs make a similar point: many would prefer to live unprotected on a roof or in the desert than in the comfort of a home run by a quarrelsome woman. By quarrelsome we mean a woman who seemingly delights in stirring up conflict—nagging, arguing, pouting, manipulating—instead of nourishing an environment of love.

Another proverb emphasizes this point. Proverbs 27:15–16 states, "A quarrelsome wife is like / a constant dripping on a rainy day; / restraining her is like restraining the wind / or grasping oil with the hand." Here Proverbs pictures a quarrelsome wife as a leaky roof. The husband comes inside to find shelter from the storm, but instead he finds no shelter at all. As one commentator put it, "...he married with the expectation of finding good, but the wife from whom he expected protection from the rudeness of the world harshly attacks him at home."[1] As we will see when we look at Proverbs 31, a wife should strive to make her home comfortable and loving for her husband and children. Proverbs offers scathing condemnation for those wives who refuse this task, and instead provide an environment only of strife.

How different this is from the wife Proverbs commends. In Proverbs 19:14 we read, "Houses and wealth are inherited from parents, but a prudent wife is from the LORD." In this instance, prudence refers to a woman who effectively manages a household with her husband—caring for the finances especially. But I think we can broaden the application to any excellent wife who provides a stable home environment: she is truly a gift from the Lord.

Proverbs elsewhere pictures this same choice—as to which type of wife you'll be (or marry)—in a vivid illustration. Proverbs 14:1 says, "The wise woman builds her house, but with her own hands the foolish one tears hers down." Every woman has a choice to make: she can either contribute to the spiritual and material well-being of her household, or she can actively destroy it. The former builds a house—a home—for herself and her family; the latter destroys any hope of having one. The choice before you as a woman is to be someone committed to the spiritual and material well-being of your family or not. Even more vividly, Proverbs 12:4 says, "A wife of noble character is her husband's crown, but a disgraceful wife is like decay in his bones." The excellent wife is her husband's crown—his most prized possession, and a visible symbol to the community of her worth. She contributes to his standing and empowers him to rule in his home. By contrast, a shameful wife robs her husband of his happiness and usefulness like a debilitating disease. The choice again becomes clear.

Proverbs does address this point with regard to women generally (not wives specifically) as well. In a memorable verse, Proverbs 11:22 reads, "Like a gold ring in a pig's snout is a beautiful woman who shows no discretion." Here, the woman takes her inner dignity (that's what the word "beautiful" is getting at—more than physical attractiveness) and tosses it aside as foolishly as sticking a beautiful ring in a pig's nose. This is an especially important verse for teenaged girls because you all will have the opportunity to throw away your dignity foolishly. Immodest dress, for example, replaces true beauty with raw sexuality and so degrades the woman dressed that way. Likewise, girls have many opportunities to trade the joy and dignity of a pure lifestyle in pursuit of momentary physical pleasures. So often, girls willingly give away their inner dignity—their "gold ring"—in order to feel loved or wanted by generally unworthy guys (pigs). What we want to say to you is, you are gold already: you are a woman of infinite worth and beauty because you are handcrafted by the most creative Being in the universe. The question is what will you do with your gold? Will you give it to pigs? Or will you offer it to God by living a life of excellence and virtue?

A Portrait of the Excellent Wife

In one of the most important chapters for women in all of Scripture, we see a picture—a portrait—of the excellent wife. Proverbs 31:10-31 forms an acrostic poem (meaning each line begins with a successive letter of the alphabet) detailing the "wife of noble character." I hope you will take the time now to read this important passage so that you will remember it as we take a short tour through the wisdom it offers.

Proverbs 31:10 introduces the topic by asking the question, "A wife of noble character who can find? She is worth far more than rubies." The Hebrew phrase for "woman of noble character" is particularly rich with meaning. The idea is a woman of strength and wealth (not in the sense of material possessions, but spiritual possessions). Other translators have "the excellent wife" or "the virtuous wife" for this verse. Such a woman, this poet assures us, is worth so much *because she is so rare*. You cannot find a woman of excellence in every house, so when you do find her, she is worth far more than mere precious jewels. (Interestingly, only one woman in the Old Testament is given this title—Ruth [read Ruth 3:11]—so we see how rare a woman like this is.)

The rest of the poem explains what makes her excellent. Instead of walking through verse by verse, we've tried to break down her character into three key areas where she excels. Those three areas are her *family*, her *home*, and her *ministry*. We're going to proceed in reverse order as we move towards the most important aspects of her life.

First, let's look at *ministry*. You may be surprised that we ranked ministry as the least important of these three areas—after all, aren't we all supposed to be ministers of Christ? Surely we are—but never at the expense of our families. In fact, this passage spends just a few short verses describing her ministry outside the home, whereas it spends a great amount of time discussing her ministry to her family. But she does minister to other women, and we don't want to ignore those verses—two in particular. First, in Proverbs 31:20 we read, "She opens her arms to the poor and extends her hands to the needy." We will discuss helping the needy in much greater depth in chapter 12, but for now suffice it to say she demonstrates compassion to those less fortunate than she. Second, Proverbs 31:26 says, "She speaks with wisdom, and faithful instruction is on her tongue." A woman of excellence can always dispense godly wisdom to those who need to hear it—her children, especially, but also her friends and neighbors. The woman of excellence fulfills the desire of Paul that the older women train the younger in godliness (Titus 2:4).

But she never does so to the neglect of her *home*, secondly. Although this is not popular in today's culture, we must acknowledge that a woman has an important role in the home—to provide a stable and loving environment for her husband, her children, and even her guests. Verse after verse describes the time and energy the woman of excellence devotes to her home. Consider, for example, Proverbs 31:13–19:

> She selects wool and flax
> and works with eager hands.
> She is like the merchant ships,
> bringing her food from afar.
> She gets up while it is still dark;
> she provides food for her family
> and portions for her servant girls.
> She considers a field and buys it;
> out of her earnings she plants a vineyard.
> She sets about her work vigorously;
> her arms are strong for her tasks.
> She sees that her trading is profitable,
> and her lamp does not go out at night.
> In her hand she holds the distaff
> and grasps the spindle with her fingers.

In these few verses, we see her devotion to the management of her household. She *works tirelessly*—"she gets up while it is still dark" and "her lamp does not go out at night." She *provides for her family*—both food and clothing (though we're not sure how many of the excellent women we know today hold a distaff or grasp a spindle). Elsewhere it says, "When it snows, she has no fear for her household; / for all of them are clothed in scarlet. / She makes coverings for her bed; / she is clothed in fine linen and purple" (Proverbs 31:21–22). She needn't fear for her children's health in winter because she knows they have the clothes they need. Similarly, she makes sure her family has all the necessary bedding. And she *completes her work with industry and efficiency*: "she sets about her work vigorously," "she sees that her trading is profitable." Truly, the woman of excellence commits herself to the betterment of her home. To summarize, we could quote Proverbs 31:27: "She watches over the affairs of her household and does not eat the bread of idleness." With diligence and commitment, she makes sure her home has what it needs to run smoothly.

Lastly, the woman of excellence devotes herself to her *family*. The woman of excellence takes care of her home because it is the environment in which her family lives—and she never forgets that the people matter more than the place. (We've seen some women much more devoted to making sure their homes look like the latest home-remodeling show than to making it a place of warmth and love for their families.) Proverbs 31:11–12 describes her relationship to her husband: "Her husband has full confidence in her / and lacks nothing of value. She brings him good, not harm, / all the days of her life." Scripture condemns humans placing trust in anyone but the Lord (consider Psalm 118:8)—but here, it commends a woman who herself so fears the Lord (Proverbs 31:30) that her husband can place his trust in her. This is truly remarkable. Her husband can place his confidence in her because he knows how she serves the Lord. Equally remarkable is the willingness of the wife to deliberately do good for her husband. Most people serve themselves first and anyone else as an afterthought. But the woman of excellence commits herself to bringing her family whatever good she can.

In the care of her children (providing the necessities of life, as we saw above), she proves exemplary as well. In fact, her devotion to her family is so great, "Her children arise and call her blessed; / her husband also, and he praises her: / 'Many women do noble things, / but you surpass them all'" (Proverbs 31:28–29). Because she commits herself to her family, her family gives her the highest praise. How different this is from children who complain about a nagging mother or a couple who bicker constantly because neither will serve the other! The woman of excellence serves as a model to women everywhere with her family, in her home, and in her ministry.

The Heart of the Matter

You may have noticed we haven't yet talked about her relationship with God. On a list of priorities, her relationship with God comes before any other—her family, her home, and her ministry. This is the heart of the matter. A woman cannot be a woman of excellence if she does not fear the Lord. In a wonderful verse, Proverbs 31:30 says, "Charm is deceptive, and beauty is fleeting; but a woman who fears the LORD is to be praised." This woman of excellence does fear the Lord—that is the beginning of wisdom, after all!—and so she receives the praise due her. You cannot devote yourself to making the perfect home, raising the perfect children, or whatever, if you have not first devoted yourself fully to God. In him is all wisdom, grace, and love—and you'll need all three to create a family!

We find it so intriguing that this poet contrasts fear of the Lord with pursuit of charm and beauty. For many women in today's culture, looking beautiful is the highest goal; it is a struggle nearly all women face. And yet, in a description of the excellent woman, outer beauty appears nowhere. All Proverbs says on this subject is "beauty is fleeting." We all grow old, so those who trust in their looks will come to ruin in the end. Likewise, "charm is deceptive." Learning to flirt, to play coy with guys, will help you about as much as your looks will. In the end, the only bedrock on which to stand is a thriving, vibrant relationship with your Maker. Ask yourself this question: do I devote myself more to fearing the Lord or to my appearance? Look at the way you spend your money—do you give more to the church and to the needy than you spend on clothes and make-up? Look at how you spend your time—do you spend as much time in prayer as you do on your hair, or as much time in the Word as you do on choosing an outfit? Charm and beauty will never get you the praise that fearing the Lord will.

Memory Verse

"Charm is deceptive, and beauty is fleeting; but a woman who fears the LORD is to be praised."
PROVERBS 31:30

Study Questions

1. What are your thoughts on gender issues? Are you willing to submit to Scripture on this point?

2. What makes a quarrelsome wife such a difficult companion?

3. Girls, what type of woman do you want to be (or, what do you want to do with your "gold")? Guys, what type of girl do you want to marry? Why?

4. What are the three key areas in which a woman of excellence excels? How does she excel in each?

5. Why is it so important to take care of the home? What is the most important part of the home?

6. What is the most important relationship a woman can have? How can you ensure that God has his rightful place in your life?

EIGHT

THE SOVEREIGN SAVIOR OF SINNERS

For all its pithy sayings, all the wisdom contained within, Proverbs makes very little mention of the Lord. The individual proverbs often seem to be generally religious—wisdom well worth keeping, even separate from a specific belief system. However, the theological framework will not allow us to see God as absent. He does not get mentioned often (although we will look at some exceptions), but the writers assume his existence and truth throughout the book. Indeed, the first nine chapters—a series of talks that a father gives to his son, imploring him to seek wisdom—seem to assume the pursuit of God. The key comes in Proverbs 9:3, where personified Wisdom "calls from the highest point of the city," asking people to come to her. In Ancient Near Eastern culture, the highest point in the city was where the most important member of that city lived—the local god. So when the Hebrews built the temple to the one true God, they built it at the highest point in Jerusalem. If Wisdom lives at the highest point in the city, then Wisdom must somehow be connected to God. In fact, some scholars even think that Wisdom represents the Holy Spirit.

So even though God's name doesn't appear very often in Proverbs, his truth pervades the whole book. But let's take a look at those places where the writers mention God explicitly. In describing our relationship to God, Proverbs highlights three main points: God is *sovereign*, God is *savior*, and we are *sinners*. We will look at each in turn—and then ask the question, "How should we respond?"

Sovereign: The Master of the Universe

According to Proverbs, God is sovereign. God controls the whole universe—his creation—and accomplishes all of his purposes in it. Nothing happens outside of God's control. Proverbs 16:4 makes this very point when it says, "The LORD works out everything for his own ends—even the wicked for a day of disaster." God has purposes and plans—"his own ends"—for the world, and he makes sure that whatever happens furthers those plans. God will see his purposes through. Ephesians 1:11 makes the same point, saying, he "works out everything in conformity with the purpose of his will." He will accomplish his will for the world. Part of this, as the verse makes clear, includes calling people to account for their actions. God will have an answer for every action. The wicked will receive their answer on an evil day—the day of disaster. Whatever happens, it happens under God's control.

God's control extends even to what we might call "chance" or "luck." Many people agree that God controls the major sweep of history, culminating in Christ's return and the creation of new heavens and a new earth. But God controls every minute detail too. Proverbs 16:33 notes, "The lot is cast into the lap, but its every decision is from the LORD." In Hebrew culture, people cast lots (not altogether unlike throwing dice) to help them make a choice. This verse suggests that God controls what numbers come up on the dice. In other words, God determines the choices that these people make.

This control even extends beyond people intentionally seeking direction by casting lots. No matter how you plan your life, ultimately God controls what happens. Proverbs 16:9 declares, "In his heart a man plans his course, but the LORD determines his steps." We all make plans for our lives. You may have plans regarding what college you want to attend or what career you want to pursue. That's fine. Making plans is a good idea. But always remember, God is in charge. He may have different plans for you, and you should accept those plans. He is a lot smarter than we are, so if he has different plans, it's for good reason! The Lord determines our steps. Actually, the Hebrew gives the singular "step" in this verse (not the plural "steps"), suggesting that God controls *each and every* move we make.

We can't take so much as a single step outside of God's control.

I saw this truth play out in my own life as a freshman in college. I had just arrived at the University of Illinois a few days earlier, and was all set to begin my time there as a Music Theory major. Unfortunately, one of the classes I needed had filled up while I waited for a proficiency exam result. Some would attribute this to bad luck, but I know differently. As a result of this scheduling debacle, I switched majors to English Literature. I know now that God intended for me to be an English major because it would help me in my ministry. I am actually teaching high school English now in Colombia—and I would have never dreamed I'd be doing that when I was a freshman in college!

God controls every aspect of this world—right down to the choices we make. "There is no wisdom, no insight, no plan that can succeed against the LORD" (Proverbs 21:30). In other words, you can't get around God's sovereignty. He *is* in control, whether we like it or not. So how should we respond to God as sovereign? Proverbs 16:3 tells us, "Commit to the LORD whatever you do, and your plans will succeed." Since God controls every step we take, we should commit our plans to him first. Make your decisions in front of the Lord, as it were. In olden days, before making important decisions—whom they planned to marry, for example—many nobles would alert their king or queen (their sovereign!) to see if they approved. In a sense, this is what we should do today with our king—the King of kings. Commit to the Lord whatever you do, to see if he approves.

A brief warning is in order here. As I mentioned earlier, Proverbs, by its very nature, gives us *principles*, not *promises*. We know this because different proverbs offer conflicting advice—the situation will determine which one proves right at that time. Take for example Proverbs 26:4–5: "Do not answer a fool according to his folly, / or you will be like him yourself. / Answer a fool according to his folly, / or he will be wise in his own eyes." Well, which is it? Should we answer a fool like a fool, or should we not? In some situations, it is better to answer a fool as a fool, so that he sees the error of his ways. In other cases, it is best not to, or else you'll make a fool of yourself. The situation determines which proves true. In the same way, Proverbs 16:3 does not offer us a promise, but a principle. Generally speaking, if you commit your plans to the Lord, you will find success. However, sometimes you will not. It may be that God has plans beyond your understanding, and that failure for a time will do more for you than immediate success would. So although we should respond to God as sovereign by committing our plans to him, we must also always *let God be God*. He knows best, and we do well to remember that.

Savior: A Tower of Refuge

God controls the universe as an absolute sovereign, but he is not an uncaring sovereign. One theologian describes God as "the king who cares,"[1] and I think he is absolutely right. God is a king, yes, but one who loves his children, protects and saves them. The writers of Proverbs saw this and made sure that we would see it too. In Proverbs 18:10, the writer assures us, "The name of the LORD is a strong tower; the righteous run to it and are safe." The image of a tower proves very evocative. It refers to a storehouse where a town or city would guard their harvest through the lean months, and it was sufficiently secure that people would take refuge within it when the town or city came under attack. In other words, God—as a tower of refuge—*provides* for and *protects* his righteous children. What a comforting thought! Trouble will come—Jesus promised us as much (John 16:33)—but God's children know they can find refuge in him at those times. People will gossip about you, but God knows the truth about you and loves you just the same (1 Corinthians 15:9–10). You will suffer pain and grief in your life, but God knows every tear that falls (Psalm 56:8) and will comfort you (Psalm 23:4). God will be a place of refuge to you when you need him. He will be a strong tower to whom you can run for protection and provision when the storms of life assail you.

How different the place of refuge of the lost! Just after Proverbs tells us that God is a strong tower, we read, "The wealth of the rich is their fortified city; they imagine it an unscalable wall" (Proverbs 18:11). If you do not trust in the Lord for your protection and comfort, where will you turn? Many turn to wealth to provide them with security—they imagine it will protect them from whatever may come, the way a fortified city protects citizens from invasion. If you know your history, though, you know that many fortified cities fell before armies (you might remember Jericho as an example). In the same way, wealth cannot provide ultimate security—it is not an "unscalable wall." Only God can provide ultimate security, because he alone is sovereign. Accomplishments, success, friends, whatever—none of these can protect and save you. Only God can.

So how should we respond to God as Savior? When facing trouble, turn to God. Take comfort in his *word* and in his *presence*, knowing that he will protect and save you. Proverbs 30:5 reminds us, "Every word of God is flawless; he is a shield to those who take refuge in him." God's Word is perfect—without error, able to accomplish all that he purposes for it—and it will bring you what you need: "teaching, rebuking, correcting and training in righteousness," so that you will be equipped for every good work (2 Timothy 3:16). Perhaps you've experienced this already. Maybe you had an issue with some friends or your parents, and God spoke to you through his proverbs in a previous chapter. You will experience it someday. When you face times of loneliness or oppression, read from the Psalms, and see if God can't speak to you through his servant David. When you feel weighed down with guilt over sin, read from Romans (chapter 8 in particular) to remember God's grace in your life. Or when you are overcome with worry and stress, read from Philippians 4 or 1 Peter 5 and throw your cares on him who cares for you. Take refuge in God's Word. When you do, his presence will shield you from the onslaught of this world.

Sinner: The One God Loves

We have looked at two aspects of our relationship to God so far: God is sovereign, and God is Savior. Basically, God is the "king who cares." In this last section, we're going to take a look at the ones God cares for—you and me. Proverbs doesn't pull punches here. It gives us the same message that the whole Bible—Genesis to Revelation—gives us: you and I are sinners in desperate need of God's grace.

Perhaps you're wondering if you're really a sinner. Maybe you think—as many people I have shared the gospel with think—you've lived a pretty good life and are probably good enough to get into heaven without God's grace. I have shared the gospel with a lot of people, and many of them tell me the same thing: "Hitler was bad, Mother Theresa was good, there's a line somewhere between them, and I'm on the right side of that line." They know they're not as good as Mother Theresa, but then, they know they're not as bad as Hitler. And they figure they're probably closer to the good than the bad, and so should wind up in heaven. Proverbs doesn't let us cling to this delusion. Proverbs 20:9 reminds us, "Who can say, 'I have kept my heart pure; I am clean and without sin'?" The point is nobody can say he kept his heart pure, and is without any sin. We have all sinned and fallen short of the glory of God (Romans 3:23). Even Mother Theresa.

See, the problem is all sin matters. Maybe you haven't killed anybody (I hope not), maybe you aren't as bad as some of your friends, but if you've sinned even once, you're facing the death penalty. Sounds harsh. Why does God care so much about sin—especially the "little" sins like lying or gossip? Well, all sin represents a breaking of the first commandment—to have no other gods before the one and only God. So you may not think your sin is that bad, but it still shows that you want to be the "god" of your life, and that is serious. But it's something we all do. So we all have to say with the writer of Proverbs, "Who can say, 'I have kept my heart pure; I am clean and without sin'?" Not me. Not you. Not anybody.

We may think we're all right, but we're not. In fact, we're so accustomed to sinning that sometimes we don't even know we're doing it. We trust ourselves, but we probably shouldn't. For, "All a man's ways seem right to him, but the LORD weighs the heart" (Proverbs 21:2). Have you ever thought you were doing something for all the right reasons, only to discover you were being selfish or thoughtless? I can remember praying as a senior in high school for a girl I knew. She was not a Christian, and I was praying that she would go to the same college where I was going so that I could "continue to share the gospel with her." (Let me share a little secret: only share the gospel with people of the same sex. Otherwise you'll create confusion like I did.) Well, the Lord answered my prayer with a resounding "No!" He knew my heart—knew that I really liked this girl—and could see that if she went to school with me, we'd probably have gotten into trouble. All my ways seemed right to me, but the Lord weighed my heart.

So how do we respond to God, knowing that we are sinners? Proverbs gives us two good responses. First, *confess your sin*. Proverbs 28:13 says, "He who conceals his sins does not prosper, but whoever confesses and renounces them finds mercy." We are all sinners. We know that. God knows that. We might as well admit it. If we don't accept the bad news, we can never really accept the good news that Christ died for our sins—so that we don't have to die eternally for them. Instead we can experience God's grace. Confess your sins and renounce them—cooperate with God's work in your life to make you more like Christ every day—and you will find mercy with God.

Second, *zealously pursue God*. Proverbs 23:17 says, "Do not let your heart envy sinners, but always be zealous for the fear of the LORD." Sometimes, as Christians, we start to get a little jealous of the world. We think people who sin without remorse are having more fun—they get to go out drinking every weekend, they have more sex (although we saw how wrong this is in the chapter on sex)... they just plain have more fun. But Proverbs reminds us not to envy them. If I were you, I wouldn't envy their fate. Read Revelation 14:14–20 and 19:17–21 for a terrifying vision of what happens to those who oppose God. Instead, be zealous for the fear of the Lord. Give him the awe and reverence he is due, especially in light of the fact that we have rebelled—and continue to rebel—against him. Seek to please him; seek to conform your life to his purpose for it. Zealously pursue God, and you will find him.

Looking Ahead

When reading the Old Testament, we must always remember that it points us to Christ. While we don't want to look for Christ lurking behind every bush, the Old Testament prepares us for the coming of Messiah through direct prophecy, the symbolism of the sacrificial system, and many other ways. Proverbs is no exception. While we have already learned that God is the sovereign Savior of sinners, what this means becomes clearer to us in the New Testament.

As the sovereign Lord, God orchestrates the events of Christ's life, especially those leading to the cross. He is even sovereign over the sinful acts of those who crucify Christ, such as Judas, Herod, and Pilate. As Luke writes, "Herod and Pontius Pilate met together with the Gentiles and the people of Israel in this city to conspire against your holy servant Jesus, whom you anointed." That much we knew. But notice the next verse: "They did what your *power* and *will* had *decided beforehand* should happen" (Acts 4:27–28, emphases added). Christ's crucifixion took place because God—in his sovereignty—decided that it be so.

Why, we might ask, would God decide for this to happen? Of course, this is because he is not only our sovereign, but also our Savior. Consider these familiar words from Paul's letter to the Romans: "God demonstrates his own love for us in this: While we were still sinners, Christ died for us" (5:7). We are sinners. We all have rebelled against a holy and perfect God, and as a consequence, we all deserve eternal death and damnation. But God, in his grace, has made a way for us. His name is Jesus, and he is the Way, the Truth, and the Life. All who enter through him are welcomed into the kingdom of God as his very sons and daughters. Hallelujah, what a Savior!

Memory Verse

"The name of the Lord is a strong tower; the righteous run to it and are safe."
Proverbs 18:10

Study Questions

1. Even though Proverbs makes little mention of God specifically, how is the whole book focused on him?

2. When we speak of God as sovereign, what does that mean he controls?

3. Why is it important to remember that Proverbs offers us principles, not promises?

4. In what ways has God provided for and protected you in your own life?

5. How has God spoken to you through his Word?

6. Have you ever experienced a time when you thought you were doing good, but in fact were serving sin? When? How did it end?

NINE

Thinking about Thinking

It makes sense to discuss attitude at the culmination of our section on relationships, because attitude will in many ways determine the health of our relationships—with God, our parents, our friends, and just about anyone. In discussing attitude, Proverbs makes one point abundantly clear: whatever else we may be, we must never be proud. Instead, we should have an attitude of humility (with other people) and fear (with God). Let's look first at the dangers of pride.

Pride: A Cancer for the Soul

Pride destroys the soul like a cancer. While Proverbs is by no means the only book of the Bible to explore the dangers of pride, it does present some interesting points. Before looking at the dangers of pride, however, we must first ask, what is pride? Pride is, at its core, an abominable self-sufficiency or self-centeredness that abandons both dependence on God and concern for others in service of self. A proud person cares neither for God's moral law nor for society's social standards. Pride elevates self to the role of god, with dire consequences. "Do you see a man wise in his own eyes? There is more hope for a fool than for him" (Proverbs 26:12). The consequences are so dire because the proud always believe themselves right, which leaves them no reason to better themselves. If you're already perfect, why change? Proverbs has very little good to say about the fool (who shuns God and wisdom), but says here that a fool has a better chance of making it than someone arrogant! At least a fool may gain wisdom, but the proud never will because they think they have it already. This is the great danger of pride.

So let's look now at why pride is so dangerous. One of the most famous proverbs says, "Pride goes before destruction, a haughty spirit before a fall" (16:18). Pride proves so dangerous because it leads inevitably to destruction. The image seems to suggest a proud someone walking down a street, nose high in the air to give off that sense of smug superiority. The trouble with keeping your nose so high in the air, though, is that you can't see the crack in the sidewalk beneath you, and so you go tumbling over. So much for pride. Now everybody's laughing at you. After pride comes the fall.

Take the imagery away now, and let's imagine it in a real-life situation. Pride usually breeds conceit, so imagine yourself bragging about how great you are at basketball or some other sport. (We'll assume you haven't learned the old joke yet, "I used to be conceited, but now I'm perfect.") What happens when someone decides to test you in this area? Suppose the new kid at school happens to be NBA-bound. If you play one-on-one, and he smokes you 21–3, what are the other kids going to say? Had you been humble, they might only have focused on how skillful the other kid is. But since you've been bragging, you can bet you'll be getting a face full of humble pie. Or imagine you've got brains instead of brawn. You have decided that since you're so smart, you don't need to study for the upcoming English test. Maybe you even mention to your friends that you don't need to study since you're such a genius. When that test comes back to you with all those red marks and that giant "D" on the top, what are your friends going to say? You should've kept your mouth shut. After pride comes the fall.

If the first main danger of pride is the inevitable fall, the second danger is damaging relationships. People don't like arrogant snobs. You probably don't like arrogant snobs, and I don't blame you. I think this may be an even greater danger than the first. If you've got your nose so high in the air that you trip and make a fool of yourself, that's probably a good thing. But if you're so stuck-up that you start damaging friendships, that's a shame. Proverbs 13:10 says, "Pride only breeds quarrels, but wisdom is found in those who take advice." We have already seen that the wise seek godly advice. Now I want to focus on the other part: pride only breeds quarrels. The proud make a real mess of relationships. Instead of listening to other people's opinions, taking their advice, respecting them as being insightful too, the proud ignore others and only listen to themselves. Not only is this foolish—as two heads really are better than one—but insulting. No one likes to feel that her opinions don't matter, but this is how the proud make all people feel. This leads to quarrels and broken friendships. After a few times of being stepped on, most people will leave a friendship; it isn't worth their staying.

You may have seen this happen in your life. Maybe you know someone in your class who always bosses people around and ridicules them for their "bad" ideas. When group project time rolls around, no one wants to work with this know-it-all. They would probably rather work with someone a little less intelligent if it means they don't have to endure the mocking. Even Hollywood—not generally known for its deep insight into the human heart—understands this point. The movie *Mean Girls* shows how one very arrogant girl pushes all of her friends away by constantly belittling them, leading to some very intense quarreling and an eventual date with the front of a school bus. Pride can make a real mess of relationships. With these dangers in mind, no wonder Proverbs asks us to consider humility as an option.

The Cure: Humility and Fear

If pride is the disease, humility is the cure. Humility is the opposite attitude from that of pride. Where pride looks to the self as the source of all knowledge and importance, humility looks outward (to others) and upward (to God). Humility depends on God for direction and grace (we might call this attitude the *fear* of the Lord) and on others for advice and support. How different this is from pride, which depends only on itself!

We have seen some of the dangers of pride already—the inevitable fall and the destruction of relationships—but what are the consequences of humility? Proverbs 22:4 tell us, "Humility and the fear of the LORD bring wealth and honor and life." An attitude of humility leads to great blessing. We can see how this proverb plays out in the life of Solomon, the man who probably penned this verse. When God came to Solomon early in his reign as king offering to grant him one request, Solomon asked for "a discerning heart to govern your people and to distinguish between right and wrong" (1 Kings 3:9). He asked this because he was humble—he said of himself, "I am only a little child and do not know how to carry out my duties." God granted his request, and was so pleased with his humility that he offered him wealth and honor as well: "I will give you what you have not asked for—both riches and honor—so that in your lifetime you will have no equal among kings" (1 Kings 3:13). The Queen of Sheba saw this when she visited Solomon's court, and remarked, "The report I heard in my own country about your achievements and your wisdom is true. But I did not believe these things until I came and saw with my own eyes. Indeed, not even half was told me; in wisdom and wealth you have far exceeded the report I heard" (1 Kings 10:6-7). Solomon's wealth and wisdom earned him his honor. So he's gotten the first two blessings of the humble life promised in Proverbs 22:4. But what about life?

God granted Solomon wealth and honor purely as a result of his humility, but he would not promise Solomon life until he proved that he feared the Lord—by keeping his commandments. God said to Solomon, "And if you walk in my ways and obey my statutes and commands as David your father did, I will give you a long life" (1 Kings 3:14). Solomon did not keep up his end of the deal—he married seven hundred women and sacrificed to their foreign gods—and so he never got to experience the fullness of life that God wants us to know. If you want wealth, honor, and life (and wealth and honor don't mean much without life), be sure to have an attitude of humility and fear. The consequences will be wonderful.

Proverbs contrasts humility and pride a number of times, in each case showing how the consequences will be much nicer with humility. We are going to look at three separate proverbs, but in each case the point will be the same: pride brings people low, but humility raises them up.

"When pride comes, then comes disgrace, but
with humility comes wisdom."
PROVERBS 11:2

"Before his downfall a man's heart is proud, but
humility comes before honor."
PROVERBS 18:12

"A man's pride brings him low, but a man of lowly spirit gains honor."
PROVERBS 29:23

When Scripture repeats an idea three times, it's a safe bet that you should pay attention. So what's God saying to us here? Pride always hurts people, whereas humility benefits them. Pride disgraces a person, causes her downfall, brings him low. Humility, contrarily, yields wisdom and honor.

Of course, the greatest example of this is Christ. Christ was famous for his humility. In fact, Paul quotes what was probably an early Christian worship song in his letter to the Philippians, praising Christ for his humility:

[He], being in very nature God,
did not consider equality with God something to be grasped,
but made himself nothing,
taking the very nature of a servant,
being made in human likeness.
And being found in appearance as a man,
he humbled himself and became obedient to death—
even death on a cross!
PHILIPPIANS 2:6–8

Christ, who deserves everything, made himself nothing. Why? Because he humbled himself in order to serve God and sinful humanity. Now, according to Proverbs, Christ should have gained honor as a result of his humility. Did this happen? Let's keep reading in Philippians:

Therefore God exalted him to the highest place
and gave him the name that is above every name,
that at the name of Jesus every knee should bow,
in heaven and on earth and under the earth,
and every tongue confess that Jesus Christ is Lord,
to the glory of God the Father. (2:9–11)

Because of his humility, Christ receives the highest praise—the worship and adoration of the entire universe. Humility brings honor, and as Paul says before quoting this song, "[O]ur attitude should be the same as that of Christ Jesus" (2:5).

The choice seems clear. Adopting an attitude of humility will help you on your way. By humbly listening to people's advice and counsel, you will gain wisdom. By concerning yourself with others instead of yourself only, you will gain honor. To boast and brag and think only of yourself, however, will sink you into the depths of despair. Disgrace will come when you discover your actions can't back up your words, the fall will come, and you will lose your standing among your peers. I hope you will choose well.

Two Steps to Take

If you've decided to choose well—to choose humility instead of pride—you may be asking yourself how you can take clear steps to help. Proverbs suggests two. First, *refuse to depend upon yourself*. Remember that God alone controls our lives, as we saw in the last chapter. Proverbs 27:1 teaches, "Do not boast about tomorrow, for you do not know what a day may bring forth." We as humans are not self-sufficient. We need to depend on God and his control in our lives. Do not make plans without consulting God, and when making plans, be sure to hold them loosely. My wife and I learned this lesson in dramatic fashion, as I can assure you we had no plans to go to Colombia when we left—in fact, one of us remarked just before leaving, "I'm not going to Colombia, and you can't make me." And yet, three months later, we were on our way; and now, four years later, here we still are. Do not boast about how secure your future is, for only

God knows what tomorrow will bring.

Second, *leave bragging to someone else.* We all feel underappreciated at one time or another, and we're likely to try to remedy that problem by making others aware of just how great we are. But nobody wants to hear it from you. People will not think more highly of you because of your boasting—they'll think the opposite. Continue to serve others humbly, and you will find that others will call attention to your excellence. As Proverbs 27:2 says, "Let another praise you, and not your own mouth; someone else, and not your own lips." There is real wisdom here. I have seen so often in the life of my wife the truth of this proverb. She has a tremendous servant's heart, yet she never calls attention to herself. As a result, people constantly praise her (as I am doing right now!). Leave the bragging to those around you. Keep an attitude of humility for yourself.

Memory Verse

"Do you see a man wise in his own eyes?
There is more hope for a fool than for him."
Proverbs 26:12

Study Questions

1. What makes pride so deadly as an attitude?

2. Have you ever "fallen" after boasting? How did it feel?

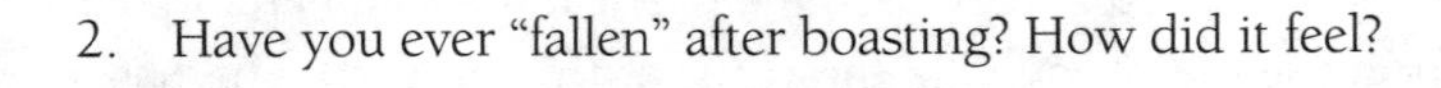

3. How can a proud spirit damage relationships?

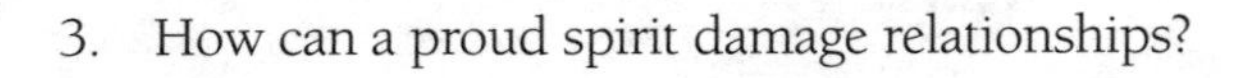

4. Why does humility bring both honor and life? How does it do this in our relationship with God? With others?

5. What steps will you take to cultivate an attitude of humility in your life?

TEN

Speaking Of...

James, in his stirring letter to the twelve tribes, warns that no one can tame the tongue (James 3:8). Despite being such a small part of our physical make-up, the tongue plays a mighty role in our daily lives. I know of no one—man or woman, Christian or not, old or young—who has complete control of the tongue. Whether spreading gossip, lying, or even just speaking an ill-timed word, all of us struggle with our speech. In this chapter we will explore the wisdom of Proverbs as it relates to speech—to gain understanding and practical tips in this monumentally important life arena. We will begin by examining the power of speech.

To Hurt or to Heal?

As Christians, we must give due consideration to our speech because it has such power. Speech has, quite frankly, the power to hurt or to heal another person. Proverbs 18:21 describes it memorably: "The tongue has the power of life and death, and those who love it will eat its fruit." Hurting and healing find their ultimate ends in death and life respectively, and this is the power the tongue has. Surely Proverbs does not mean merely literal life and death, but all forms of health or harm. The tongue has the power to kill community, for example, if someone viciously attacks another member of a church youth group. We have all seen parents or teachers killing a child's spirit by embarrassing them, killing their dreams by belittling them. The tongue also has the power to heal, though. A kind word given at the right time can uplift someone for days afterwards—a genuine comment on appearance, a job well done, or whatever. A word of encouragement can propel someone forward onto a seemingly unattainable goal just as easily as a word of discouragement can keep them from trying. The tongue has the power of life and death.

The next part of the proverb simply means that those who choose their words carefully—who "love" the tongue—will reap the benefit, whether good or bad. Some people very carefully consider their words in order to bless another as much as possible. Such people will eat the fruit of blessing—seeing the smile on the person's face, winning friends, gaining a hearing wherever they go. Others choose their words just as carefully, but intend to wound the other person, to embarrass someone else to make themselves feel better. Such people also eat the fruit of their speech: losing friends, having an empty self-esteem, living with the knowledge that they have caused another to suffer.

Though never quite as poignantly, Proverbs emphasizes the power of the tongue in two other places. First, Proverbs 12:18 says, "Reckless words pierce like a sword, but the tongue of the wise brings healing." Again, words have the power to injure another person—and in many ways the injury is worse than a physical injury. Swords can do great damage—they will probably leave a scar forever—but so can words. A wise person, however, uses his or her words to bring healing. Everyone we meet will bear wounds from other people—from parents, friends, and enemies. The wise among us will use the great power God has given us—the power of speech—to bring healing to those people.

Second, Proverbs 15:4 notes, "The tongue that brings healing is a tree of life, but a deceitful tongue crushes the spirit." Those who use the power of speech are like trees whose fruit is life itself. People come to these "trees" to eat of the fruit that will enliven them. Wouldn't you like to be the type of person that people come to for refreshment and encouragement? The other type of person—the deceitful tongue, which we'll get to in a moment—crushes the spirit of other people.

A Test Case: The Power of the Tongue

I have just argued that speech is very powerful—but am I right? Let's look at a test case to see the tongue's power. Proverbs 15:1 says, "A gentle answer turns away wrath, but a harsh word stirs up anger." Here we see the power of speech. Imagine a situation in which emotions are starting to run high. Some type of misunderstanding is brewing between you and another person. That person has come to you to confront you, and voices are starting to rise. What do you do? You have two choices, and each demonstrates the power of the tongue. You could give a gentle answer—accept responsibility and express a desire to resolve the conflict peacefully. This answer will turn away wrath, according to Proverbs. Disaster has been averted. But you could also give a harsh word—tell the person to back off and shut up, or some other nonsense. What happens then? You have stirred up anger the way someone stirs up a dying fire. The tongue has great power—to hurt or to heal—depending on how you use it.

The Apt Word

Before we move on, I want to discuss one more aspect of the tongue's power: the apt word. An apt word is just the right word given at just the right time. Sometimes you will meet someone who needs to hear something very particular—a challenge, a word of encouragement, some sympathy. Proverbs says these words are "like apples of gold in settings of silver" (Proverbs 25:11); that is, they have great wealth and value. Proverbs 15:23 makes the same point: "A man finds joy in giving an apt reply—and how good is a timely word!" The right word given at the right time is something very precious, so precious that it even brings joy to the person giving it. I know I have been humbly overjoyed to find that I had the words someone needed to hear. So when you encounter someone who needs an apt word, be ready to give it.

To Be Wise or Foolish?

Just as our speech forces us to make a choice between hurting and healing, so it forces us to choose between being wise or foolish. Perhaps nothing reveals us to be one or the other quite so much as our speech. A fool need only open his mouth to prove to the world he's a fool. Proverbs 15:2 says, "The tongue of the wise commends knowledge, but the mouth of the fool gushes folly." Those who speak wisely make knowledge seem enticing. Maybe you've had a teacher who spoke so eloquently and gently concerning an issue that she caught your attention and made you want to learn more about it. Wise people make wisdom seem worthwhile. Fools, on the other hand, do nothing but multiply foolishness. They seem to be like a dam bursting, except foolish thoughts and words pour out instead of water. In both cases, the speech makes clear what type of person is speaking. So let's compare for a moment how each speaks and the resulting consequences. We'll begin with the fool.

The Fool

The fool loves to talk despite the fact that he says nothing of value. Proverbs 18:2 notes, "A fool finds no pleasure in understanding but delights in airing his own opinions." The fool doesn't bother to learn about what he's talking about; she just loves to talk—to hear the melodious sound of her voice. Unfortunately, this holds true for many teenagers. They love to talk about grown-up issues—politics, religion, morality—but rarely take the time to research or study the issues first. (Even sadder, most adults don't bother to either.)

What happens to such people? Three proverbs all point in the same direction. First, "A fool's lips bring him strife, and his mouth invites a beating" (Proverbs 18:6). Fools end up getting into trouble. In fact, they make their own trouble. The first part of the proverb suggests that fools stir up controversy, but the second part tells us that it backfires. They start the problem, but someone else finishes it—probably with a fist to the mouth. Second, "A fool's mouth is his undoing, and his lips are a snare to his soul" (Proverbs 18:7). This proverb continues the idea from the previous verse, but informs us that the fool's foolish talk leads to untimely death. Genuine fools don't just make trouble… they make big trouble. I hope none of you will speak so foolishly as to invite death, but remember, words have power! It could happen.

In light of these two verses, I hope you would prefer to speak wisely rather than foolishly. Our third proverb illuminating the consequences of foolish talk shows us a better way. "A fool's talk brings a rod to his back, but the lips of the wise protect them" (Proverbs 14:3). Fools get punished for speaking foolishly. Back then, this meant getting whipped. These days, it might mean getting a detention or getting fired. In any case, the fool didn't need to suffer this punishment; they bring it on themselves. Much smarter, it seems to me, to be wise—knowing that wise speech will protect you.

The Wise

The wise face consequences for their speech as surely as fools do, but the consequences are good. We have already seen that the lips of the wise protect them. What other consequences do the wise face for their speech? Basically, wise speech invites respect and high esteem. If you speak wisely, people will start listening to you. Proverbs 20:15 says, "Gold there is, and rubies in abundance, but lips that speak knowledge are a rare jewel." When people see a rare jewel, they stop and look. One of the main tourist attractions in Bogotá is the Gold Museum. This whole museum dedicates itself to presenting the delicate and valuable gold crafts from pre-Colombian civilizations. People want to see gold and jewels. But lips that speak knowledge—these are rarer still. If you speak wisely, people will admire you for your wisdom in the same way tourists admire the artifacts at the Gold Museum.

Not only will people admire you for your wisdom, but if you speak wisely, people will listen to you. They will pay attention to your words and make changes based on them. Prove yourself trustworthy, and you might even find your parents or teachers listening to and implementing your ideas. Proverbs 25:15 says, "Through patience a ruler can be persuaded, and a gentle tongue can break a bone." I have, thank goodness, never broken any bones beyond some toes—but not for a lack of trying. I play soccer regularly, along with football, basketball, waterskiing, and hiking. I have had opportunity to break bones, but it has never happened, because bones are hard to break. They are meant to be durable. And yet Proverbs tells us that a gentle tongue can break a bone. This image presents the idea that wise speech—gentle, persuasive words—can break even durable opposition. Eventually, people—even rulers—will listen to the ideas you have, if you present them wisely.

To Speak or Not to Speak?

The tongue has great power—to hurt or to heal, to prove someone wise or foolish—and so it is best to use it sparingly. Many proverbs speak of the wisdom in remaining silent or at least listening carefully before responding. To begin, Proverbs lists three reasons why we ought to speak but little: to keep us from sin, to keep us from trouble, and to keep us from looking foolish. First, *to keep us from sin*: Proverbs 10:19 says, "When words are many, sin is not absent, but he who holds his tongue is wise." Because it is so hard to tame the tongue, speaking much will lead inevitably to sinning. People who talk too much will find themselves saying what they shouldn't—gossip, lies, hurtful comments, or just plain foolishness. The wise person, then, holds his tongue in order to keep from sinning. If you were to keep from speaking all day long someday (which isn't a bad idea—it's called the discipline of silence), I guarantee you that you wouldn't sin with your speech that day. Simple.

Second, *to keep us from trouble*: Proverbs 21:23 says, "He who guards his mouth and his tongue keeps himself from calamity." We saw above that foolish talk usually leads to some kind of trouble. People who choose their words carefully—and therefore use their words sparingly—will save themselves much of this type of trouble. Pretend your mouth is a prison, housing all sorts of convicts (your sinful words). Make sure you post some guards at the door so those convicts don't get out. I am sure you have all experienced at some point in your life that scourge of the earth—foot-in-mouth disease. That is what happens when you say something without thinking and then immediately regret having said it. To prevent that calamity, guard your speech.

Third, *to keep us from looking like a fool*: Proverbs 17:28 says, "Even a fool is thought wise if he keeps silent, and discerning if he holds his tongue." You may be a tremendous fool, but since our words so often are the culprits that betray our foolishness, no one will know if you don't say anything! Maybe you've witnessed one of those amusing conversations where, when several people are discussing a difficult topic, someone tries to enter the conversation only to realize he isn't nearly smart enough to participate in it. If you've seen the movie *Bridget Jones' Diary*, you may recall such a scene involving a discussion of literature. Bridget would have been wise to keep her mouth shut, and often we would be wise to do the same. When you keep quiet while everyone else is yammering away, people will think you contemplative and thoughtful—instead of a fool.

Speaking Hastily

In addition to encouraging us to speak but little, Proverbs suggests we refrain from speaking hastily too. People who answer too quickly—before they understand the whole issue—often speak foolishly. Proverbs 18:13 warns, "He who answers before listening—that is his folly and his shame." Before pronouncing judgment on an issue publicly, be sure you have heard all there is to hear on the subject. You may have decided that one friend was clearly in the wrong in some situation, only to discover later that you didn't have all the facts. Get all the facts before you tell people what you think, and you'll save yourself the embarrassment of making a public mistake. To answer before listening will bring you only folly and shame.

Likewise, Proverbs 29:20 says, "Do you see a man who speaks in haste? There is more hope for a fool than for him." Speaking without thinking always means speaking foolishly. Fools don't think much—so people who skip that vital step sound like fools. People who don't apply wisdom to their speech end up making fools of themselves. Their fate will be no better than that of a fool.

Speaking with Restraint

If speaking hastily is the problem, speaking with restraint is the solution. Proverbs 13:3 sets the contrast before us: "He who guards his lips guards his life, but he who speaks rashly will come to ruin." Guarding our lips—carefully considering what we will say—means guarding our well-being. Speaking rashly, as we've seen, leads only to ruin. A wise man gives thought to his words as surely as he gives thought to his steps. He restrains himself from speaking hastily. Proverbs 17:27 says, "A man of knowledge uses words with restraint, and a man of understanding is even-tempered." Especially when facing provocation, a wise person will restrain herself from speaking—too quickly, at least, but possibly from speaking at all. Such people are "cool" under pressure—calm, rational, even-tempered—instead of being hot-headed. So not only should we speak but little, but when we do speak, we need to make sure it is slowly and calmly, never hastily.

Two Final Areas

Now that we've looked at three choices to make when speaking—to hurt or heal, to be wise or foolish, to speak much or little—let's examine two final areas that matter enormously in our speech: truth and gossip. We will begin with truth.

The Truth, the Whole Truth...

...and nothing but the truth. That is the standard for Christians, and it is a standard to which Proverbs holds us. Proverbs 6:16–19—a passage startling in its directness—alerts us as to why telling the truth matters so much.

> There are six things the LORD hates,
> seven that are detestable to him:
> haughty eyes,
> a *lying tongue,*
> hands that shed innocent blood,
> a heart that devises wicked schemes,
> feet that are quick to rush into evil,
> *a false witness who pours out lies*
> and a man who stirs up dissension among brothers. (Emphasis added)

Interestingly, two of the seven things the Lord hates have to do with truth-telling—the two phrases in italics. God hates a lying tongue and a false witness who pours out lies. Apparently, telling the truth matters to God. If for no other reason than this, one ought to avoid telling lies. And in case we missed so bold a declaration, Proverbs repeats it: "The LORD detests lying lips, but he delights in men who are truthful" (Proverbs 12:22). Again we learn that God detests the lips of those who lie. But here we see the opposite truth too. God delights in those who tell the truth. Truth matters to God, and it ought to matter to us too.

God is not the only one who delights in those who are truthful. Other people respect and appreciate those who are honest. In fact, Proverbs 24:26 says, "An honest answer is like a kiss on the lips." A kiss is one of the most intimate acts between people—a man and his wife, a parent and child, even between friends (I live in a culture where friends kiss on the cheek regularly). Proverbs connects telling the truth to a kiss because both reflect intimacy and a strengthening of the relationship. To lie repeatedly to someone will feel like a slap in the face, destroying any hope of a relationship. But to tell the truth consistently will draw you closer together.

Knowing that God and other people care about the truthfulness of our speech ought to be motivation enough to be honest. If this has not convinced you, however, consider the consequences of your speech. Proverbs 26:28 warns us, "A lying tongue hates those it hurts, and a flattering mouth works ruin." If truth-telling fosters intimacy, lying fosters only hurt—and reflects hatred toward the other person. Flattery—deceiving another for the sake of personal gain—will eventually lead to ruin. I have known several girls who were deeply hurt as a result of flattery. Many men will use charm and flattery—insincere compliments about appearance normally—to woo a girl so that they can have their way with them physically. This inevitably leaves the girl in ruins, feeling hurt and used, and deadens the soul of the man. Lying to parents—about where you were or what you did over the weekend, for example—will hurt them deeply when they discover the truth. They will feel betrayed, and the relationship will suffer. Lying only leads to ruin.

Perpetual lying will eventually destroy a person's life, as no one can trust a habitual liar. Proverbs 12:19 presents us with a choice: "Truthful lips endure forever, but a lying tongue lasts only a moment." Those who tell the truth will continue on their course, earning the respect of others and the favor of God. Those who lie will soon find themselves lost—the lie lasts but a moment once the truth is discovered, and God will destroy them in the blink of an eye. Better to tell the truth, I would think. For the sake of your relationships—with God as well as other people—commit to tell the truth always.

Gossip: Cancer of the Tongue

Cancer may not be a strong enough image for how damaging gossip can be. Gossips decide to spread slanderous rumors—whether ultimately true or not—in order to win friends and destroy others. Gossip cares little for the truth—a frightening thought, considering how much God cares for the truth—and cares instead for the pleasure of the moment. What makes gossip so dangerous—apart from the damage it does to the one being talked about—is how good it feels to do. It feels good to hear gossip, and it feels good to pass on gossip. Watch the next time someone starts to share gossip. Everyone else present will lean in and get a very interested look on their faces. People love gossip. Proverbs describes it this way, "The words of a gossip are like choice morsels; they go down to a man's inmost parts" (Proverbs 18:8). Gossip is like dessert—everybody wants some, and nothing tastes quite so good going down.

And yet gossip does so much damage. Gossip targets unsuspecting victims—people who often don't know they're being talked about, and who can't defend themselves with truth—and destroys them in an instant among a whole crowd of people. No wonder Proverbs says, "Without wood a fire goes out; without gossip a quarrel dies down" (Proverbs 26:20). Gossip keeps the fires of interpersonal conflict raging, the same way fresh wood keeps a fire burning. Scripture implores us to love one another, but when we gossip, we do the exact opposite.

We must commit to curing the cancer of gossip in our lives. The two principles for doing this are easy to understand but so very difficult to apply. First, *refuse to share gossip about anyone*. What you share may be true or it may be rumor, but if it will harm another person's reputation, refuse to tell anyone about it. In your life you will learn dirty secrets about many people. Except in very specific circumstances—someone seeking to be an elder or pastor, for example, where hidden secrets can damage the whole church—never share those secrets. Confront that person, as we talked about in our chapter on friendship, but do not confront other people with the sad truth. A wise rule would be if it seems important enough to tell someone else about it—that is, if you are tempted to gossip about it—it is important enough to tell God about it (prayer) and the person involved (confrontation) instead. Second, *refuse even to listen to gossip*. Do not be a willing accomplice to gossip. If there aren't any ears to listen, people will stop sharing gossip. Establish a reputation as someone who detests gossip. In fact, don't even just stop listening, but confront the person sharing the gossip too. Gossip is a terrible sin. You have a choice—to be someone trustworthy or to be a gossip. Remember, "A gossip betrays a confidence, but a trustworthy man keeps a secret" (Proverbs 11:13). What's it going to be?

Memory Verse

"The tongue has the power of life and death, and those who love it will eat its fruit."
Proverbs 18:21

Study Questions

1. How do words have the power of life and death?

2. Recall a time when someone spoke a harsh or a kind word to you. What was the outcome? How did you feel?

3. Has anyone ever given you an "apt word"? When? How did it serve you?

4. What consequences does foolish talk bring? What about wise speech?

5. Why is telling the whole truth so important?

6. What makes gossip so dangerous? Have you ever experienced hurt from gossip? Have you ever hurt others?

ELEVEN

Sleeping and Sluggards

Senioritis. It's an issue we all face in school. If you're like me, it's an issue you started to face sometime around your freshmen year—which makes me wonder about the name. We all face the terrible temptation to be lazy. It is just plain easier to recline on the couch, checking to see what's on the idiot box, than to do anything of any benefit to society. But Proverbs has something to say about this too.

The Sluggard

Most of the proverbs that address laziness describe the personality and actions of the sluggard—the lazy guy. These proverbs are intended not just as a description—how to spot one in your neighborhood—but as a warning, so that you won't become one yourself (or, if you are one already, so that you'll change your ways). So let's turn first to the personality of the sluggard.

Personality

The sluggard has certain set personality traits. Wherever you find these traits, you are sure to find someone lazy. First, the sluggard *rationalizes his or her laziness*. That is, the sluggard can always find some excuse for being lazy rather than working hard. Look at Proverbs 22:13: "The sluggard says, 'There is a lion outside!' or, 'I will be murdered in the streets!'" Why does the sluggard fear being eaten alive or murdered in the streets? Simple. If there is some danger lurking outside your door, you would be wise to remain indoors. If you knew there was a mugger waiting on your doorstep, you would never dream of going outside. You would wait inside until he left, and to pass the time while waiting, you might start flipping through the channels on TV. The sluggard wants to sit on her couch watching TV, so she assumes that danger must be outside. If some imaginary danger exists—getting hit by a car, struck by lightning, or eaten by a pack of rabid hamsters—then she has the perfect excuse for doing nothing that day. The sluggard rationalizes his or her laziness.

Second, the sluggard *ignores opportunity*. Opportunity may come knocking on the sluggard's door, but the sluggard is too drained to answer it. Consider Proverbs 19:24: "The sluggard buries his hand in the dish; he will not even bring it back to his mouth!" Now this proverb uses hyperbole—exaggeration—to make its point. Most people, if they've gone through all the work of preparing a meal, would probably want to enjoy it. And even if you didn't make the meal, if you've already got your hand in the nachos, you're liable to bring it back up again. Most sluggards would do this much. But the point is that sluggards start something, but never finish it. Even when one has his hand in the dish, so to speak, he won't take advantage of the opportunity before him.

Sluggards start filling out scholarship applications, but they never finish them. Sluggards join a health club, but they never bother to exercise there. Sluggards bring their backpacks home with them, but can never quite get around to doing the extra credit assignment (or even just the homework). The sluggard ignores opportunity.

Third, the sluggard *frustrates those around him or her*. Whenever people have to work with a sluggard, they end up getting mad. Proverbs 10:26 says, "As vinegar to the teeth and smoke to the eyes, so is a sluggard to those who send him." If you've ever been around a campfire, you know how irritating smoke in the eyes can be. And if you've never done it before, pour yourself a glass of vinegar and drink it down in under three seconds. (Okay, let me save you from this one—it doesn't taste too good. You'll probably throw up.) This is how people see a sluggard. He irritates them. Why? Because he doesn't do his work. If you send a guy on an errand and he never does it, you're probably going to be upset. That's the idea. This is the person in every group project at school who doesn't do his or her share of the work. You divide up who's going to do what, and everybody gets their jobs done... except one. If you've been in a group with that guy, you know how irritating it can be. Don't be that guy. The sluggard frustrates those around him or her.

Actions

I should probably say "inactions," but oh well. We have seen the sluggard's personality. Now let's take a look at what he does. First—and not surprisingly—the sluggard *does nothing*. This seems obvious. The whole idea behind being lazy is doing nothing. And sure enough, the sluggard does nothing better than anyone. Read Proverbs 6:9–11:

> How long will you lie there, you sluggard?
> When will you get up from your sleep?
> A little sleep, a little slumber,
> a little folding of the hands to rest—
> and poverty will come on you like a bandit
> and scarcity like an armed man.

The sluggard sleeps soundly with no care for what tomorrow brings; and so when tomorrow comes, he finds himself poor. People who don't work hard in school don't get into college; people who don't show up for work don't get paid. It is a simple idea in theory, but in practice it can be much more difficult. The sluggard does nothing.

Second, the sluggard *makes no progress*. She doesn't just do nothing—she makes an art of it. As Proverbs 26:14 says, "As a door turns on its hinges, so a sluggard turns on his bed." Now, think about the door for a minute. For all its movement, how much progress does a door make? Not so much. It is fixed on its hinges. It can't get anywhere. In the same way, the sluggard's movement yields no real progress—probably because it only involves turning over in bed. Both the door and the sluggard are stuck where they started, anchored where they've always been. But the door is stuck there by design, whereas the sluggard is there by choice. Sluggards make no progress.

Third, the sluggard *refuses to plan ahead.* Proverbs is filled with wisdom about planning for the future, but sluggards ignore this wisdom. They let each day bring what it may... with disastrous consequences. "A sluggard does not plow in season; so at harvest time he looks but finds nothing" (Proverbs 20:4). Farming is not a difficult concept. You plant at the right time, and then you harvest at the right time. The trouble is, if you forget step one (planting), you're not going to have much to do when it comes to step two (harvesting). This is the idea behind Proverbs 20:4. If you don't plant, you won't be able to harvest anything—which means you'll probably starve to death. Sluggards don't think that far ahead, though. They prefer to live in a dream world where actions (or lack thereof) have no consequences. Sluggards don't do homework and then can't figure out why they didn't pass ninth grade. Sluggards don't save their money but don't know why they can't afford to go on that ski trip coming up. Sluggards give no thought to the future, only to what seems best right now. Sluggards refuse to plan ahead.

A Study in Contrasts

While Proverbs offers us a broad overview of the sluggard, many of the individual verses contrast the sluggard with the diligent. The ways in which each works—and thinks—and the consequences each faces make for an interesting study in contrasts. Let's walk through these four contrasts in turn.

First, and most obviously, the lazy and the diligent differ in their *economic stability.* There are other causes of poverty besides laziness, as even Proverbs grants, but surely laziness may be one reason for it. Proverbs 10:4 makes the clearest contrast: "Lazy hands make a man poor, but diligent hands bring wealth." Quite simply, if you don't work, you won't earn money. On the other hand, working hard will normally bring economic stability. Most people who set their minds to work end up making a decent living. Proverbs 14:23 makes the same point in a slightly different way. It says, "All hard work brings a profit, but mere talk leads only to poverty."

Here the difference is not between lazy and diligent hands, but between *work* and *talk*. The diligent may devise certain plans, but they see them through. In contrast, the lazy never get past dreaming up get-rich-quick schemes. They never put the plan into practice and so never earn the money. The lazy may talk about getting rich, but only the diligent will actually bring home the bacon.

Second, the lazy and the diligent differ in their *position in society*. Because people get frustrated with the sluggard, they can never achieve a high position at work or school. You are not going to promote someone that you regard as smoke in your eyes. The diligent, however, will often ascend the ranks of a company or organization quickly, because people know they are dependable. "Diligent hands will rule, but laziness ends in slave labor" (Proverbs 12:24). The dependable—the diligent—will be given more and more responsibility, because everyone knows they will see the task through to the end. Maybe you've heard the saying, "Don't make fun of nerds; they'll be your boss someday." That's exactly what this proverb means. "Nerds" tend to be diligent, and so they tend to run the companies where you might work. But the lazy will sink lower and lower—never able to keep a job or finish a task—until eventually they accumulate so much debt that, in the Hebrew culture, they would become slaves. (Make no mistake: massive debt represents slavery for us today, too.) The lazy sink lower while the diligent ascend ever higher.

Third, the lazy and the diligent differ in their *satisfaction with life*. Some may think that the lazy have more fun—after all, they spend the day sleeping and playing video games. While this may be true for a weekend or two—the diligent kid spends all weekend working on a major homework assignment, whereas the lazy kid procrastinates so that he can hang out at the mall—ultimately, the diligent one will get more satisfaction out of life. For, "The sluggard craves and gets nothing, but the desires of the diligent are fully satisfied" (Proverbs 13:4). Why are the desires of the diligent fully satisfied? Simple. They can afford to purchase what they desire. If you work hard, you get more money. We saw that already. And if you have enough money, you can buy the electric guitar you've always wanted, or go out to the movies with your friends. The lazy can't do that. They never bothered to earn any money in the first place, so they can't afford to make their desires come true. Of course, this has to do with far more than just money, too. Those who are diligent in their walk with God—pursuing the spiritual disciplines, zealous in prayer and study, and the like—find the deepest joy in knowing Christ and being known by him. And this is a far deeper desire than anything with a price tag, I hope!

Fourth, the lazy and the diligent differ in the *obstacles they face.* In pursuit of those desires we talked about in the last chapter, some people will find the path straight and level, whereas others will find it steep and choked with obstacles. Proverbs 15:19 says, "The way of the sluggard is blocked with thorns, but the path of the upright is a highway." If you've ever been hiking in the wilderness, you probably know the difficulty of trying to walk where there isn't much of a path. It can be hard enough to walk with logs and weeds covering the path. But it gets much, much worse when you discover that you're actually walking through a patch of something thorny—because now not only can you not walk easily, but it hurts too. This is how life is for the lazy. Because of choices they've made—not to work hard in school, for example—they find their path choked with obstacles: colleges that reject them, companies that don't want to hire them. If you've ever seen the pain on someone's face when he discovers he can't go to the school where he wants to go, you know how sharp these thorns can be. But the diligent person doesn't suffer this pain. He is on Easy Street. He puts in the effort early, and now can saunter on down the road towards his goals.

There are tremendous differences between the lazy and the diligent. Proverbs doesn't explain these differences to us for the sake of classification—how to tell the difference between a slacker and a hard worker. Proverbs explains the differences to offer us a choice. We can choose to become like the sluggard, or we can devote ourselves to diligence. Thanks to the wisdom of Proverbs, we now know what each choice entails. Yes, being diligent requires hard work—and maybe missing out on some fun along the way. But work brings reward, and you will reap that reward for the rest of your life if you continue on the path of diligence. So what's it going to be: hard work or heartbreak?

Some Practical Tips

Of course, it takes more than someone telling you to work hard to get everything done—or else all the parental nagging we endure would make us straight-A students! Here are a couple of time-tested ideas to help you get on the right track. First, *set goals* for yourself. Everyone works harder when they know what they're working towards. If you decide you want to attend a specific college, you will work harder in school. If you want to make the varsity soccer team as a sophomore, you will practice more. If you try to memorize the whole New Testament by the time you graduate from college (a great goal, and not even too difficult!), you'll keep up with your weekly memorization. Set goals for yourself, and you'll soon find yourself reaching them.

Second, *plan ahead*. Many teenagers never bother to think about the future. If they know they don't have any homework due on Monday, they'll spend the whole weekend watching TV and hanging out with friends. But then they remember Monday night at 7:00 P.M. that they have a five-page paper due on Tuesday. Had they planned ahead, they could have knocked off two or three pages over the weekend and had a much better night's sleep Monday night. A little planning can save a lot of pain.

Third, *establish priorities*. As humans, we naturally do what we want to do most. I like English and hate math, so I'm far more likely to do my English homework before ever cracking my math book. I discovered in college that I would get far ahead in some classes while getting behind in the ones I didn't like. We can't always do what we *want* to do; sometimes we have to do what we *need* to do. So, at the beginning of every day or every week, make a to-do list in order of priority. Don't start on item #2 until you've crossed off #1. This will guarantee that you take care of all your priorities in any given week.

Finally, *keep track of your time*. Set up a simple chart—broken down into half-hour increments—and note how you spend your time for a week or so. Soon you'll see where your time gets wasted. I counseled a student who couldn't figure out why she wasn't getting her homework done. I asked her to tell me about her schedule. She explained how packed her schedule was (and it was busy)—until about 6:30 p.m. At that point, she trailed off in her story. It seems she didn't really accomplish anything other than watching some TV and chatting on instant messenger after dinner. That's a lot of wasted time. If you're feeling overwhelmed with your schedule, keep track of your time to see if you're wasting time somewhere, too.

A Final Lesson: The Ant

In case you missed all the other wisdom on this subject, Proverbs presents one final lesson on laziness: the ant. Proverbs is one of the few books of the Bible that draws lessons from the natural world, but the wisdom it discovers there is well worth learning. Here is Proverbs 6:6-8:

> Go to the ant, you sluggard;
> consider its ways and be wise!
> It has no commander,
> no overseer or ruler,
> yet it stores its provisions in summer
> and gathers its food at harvest."

The ant is a model of diligence, and so the writer asks us to learn from it—that we might become wise. What makes the ant so smart? Two things.

First, the ant doesn't need someone to tell it that it should be working. It knows that already. It gets its work done without being hounded all of the time. Now many of you probably wish your mom would stop nagging you about getting your homework done or finishing a project around the home. Let me let you in on a little secret: she'll stop nagging you if you get the work done. And she'll probably be even more impressed if you start getting your work done without being told so many times. That is the lesson of the ant. Hard work brings its own reward—trust, responsibility, satisfaction—so you shouldn't need any external motivation to get it done.

Second, the ant sees the consequences of its actions. Without being told, the ant stores food all summer long. Then, when winter comes, it has all the food it needs. The ant knows—without being told—that if it doesn't store any food, it will starve to death. The ant sees the consequences of its actions, and makes sure that he brings about the consequences he wants—plenty of food over the winter. Think about it this way: you've got all summer long to hang out at the pool, or you could spend at least some of that time working. What are the consequences? In the first, you get a wicked cool tan. But then you can't have any fun all year long because you don't have any money. In the second, you still get a pretty sweet tan, but you can also catch a flick every now and again because you managed to save some money for those lean winter months. Take a look at the consequences.

What's it going to be? Hard work or heartbreak?

Memory Verse

"Lazy hands make a man poor, but diligent hands bring wealth."
Proverbs 10:4

Study Questions

1. In what areas of your life do you struggle with laziness?

2. Do you share any personality traits with the sluggard?

3. How does the image of a door swinging on its hinges capture the actions of a sluggard perfectly?

4. What are some of the differences between the lazy and the diligent? Which one better describes you? Which do you want to be? What will you do to get there?

5. What lessons did you learn from the ant?

TWELVE

MONEY MATTERS

You may wonder what I could possibly have to say to teens about money, since the only problem most teens face is not having enough of it. After all, mowing lawns, babysitting, or flipping burgers doesn't bring in the big bucks. Still, money is one of the most important issues you will face in your life. How we handle our money is so important that the Bible speaks about money even more than it speaks of love! An issue this important deserves our attention. And the godly patterns we establish when younger (and poorer) will help us make better decisions when we are older. We are going to look at four crucial concerns with money in this chapter: how much money is enough, honesty, our attitude toward the poor, and giving. Let's begin by asking the question, how much money is enough?

THE IDEAL INCOME

Before we really answer this question, I want us to pause and remember money's relative worth. For many in the world today, money is a god—even *the* god. With money you can make your dreams come true. There is nothing worse than being poor, nothing better than being rich. This is not a biblical perspective, however. Scripture almost always casts a skeptical eye on wealth, and we would do well to do likewise. Proverbs 11:4 gives us a helpful perspective on wealth: "Wealth is worthless in the day of wrath, but righteousness delivers from death." When it comes right down to it, money cannot help you at all in the most important issue you face in life:

your relationship with God. Far better to be poor and close to God than rich and spiritually dead. Money can't save your soul; a right relationship with God can. With that in mind, let's look at what Proverbs says about the ideal income.

Proverbs does not agree with the world on this issue. Most people would prefer to earn as much money as possible. But Proverbs tells us that many things are more valuable than money. Three proverbs in particular make this point by contrasting wealth with something significantly more valuable. Proverbs 15:16 says, "Better a little with the fear of the LORD than great wealth with turmoil." You may be rich, but that doesn't guarantee that your life won't be in shambles. (If you know anything about celebrities, you know how true this can be!) At the same time, many people who have very little material wealth have a deep and profound happiness because of their relationship with God. Where I attended church for a time in Bosa, one of the poorest barrios in Bogotá, I know of several families who live on little more than a few dollars a day, but who radiate joy and zeal for life. This stands in stark contrast to many of the families I knew as a child. I grew up in one of the wealthiest areas of the United States and knew many families with more money than I could ever have imagined. Most of these families ended in broken marriages, with kids on drugs or expelled from school. As one commentator says about this verse, "poverty with spiritual gain is better than spiritual poverty with economic gain."[1]

In the very next verse we read, "Better a meal of vegetables where there is love than a fattened calf with hatred" (Proverbs 15:17). Here, Proverbs compares two families—one poor and loving, the other rich and hateful. The writer basically says, I'd rather have a simple meal of vegetables than the most elaborate spread—filet mignon, baked potatoes, chocolate cake for desert—provided I can eat the meal in an environment of love rather than hate. Familial love provides far more nourishment than mere food could ever provide. Sure, we all want enough money to be able to feed our families, but we must remember that love matters more than all the wealth in the world.

Proverbs 17:1 makes a similar point: "Better a dry crust with peace and quiet than a house full of feasting, with strife." Again, the contrast centers around two meals—in this case a feast versus some bread crust. I have a friend who grew up on ketchup sandwiches—little more than a bread crust dipped in ketchup. But he grew up with a loving family, and so he wouldn't trade his childhood for all the gourmet meals in the world. Having a sporty car, the fastest computer, all the clothes you can want, the latest video game system, a plasma TV—none of this will matter if you don't have love and peace in your home. Remember, money may help you buy a few things, but the most important things in life are worth far more than what money could ever purchase.

If money can't buy the most important things in life, how much time and energy should we give to earn it? Proverbs can help guide us here too: "Do not wear yourself out to get rich; have the wisdom to show restraint" (Proverbs 23:4). We all have to work to earn money (remember the last chapter), but none of us should wear ourselves out trying to bring home the bacon. The wise person earns enough to provide the necessities in life, while remembering that spending time at home with family, cultivating a vibrant walk with God, and serving at church are all activities worthy of our best time and energy.

Of course, devoting yourself first to God, your family, and your friends may mean you miss out on earning the really big bucks. But Proverbs teaches that being rich should never be our goal in life. Rather, we should strive to earn enough to provide the necessities in life and no more. Proverbs 30:7–9 records the prayer of Lemuel on this matter:

> Two things I ask of you, O LORD;
> do not refuse me before I die:
> Keep falsehood and lies far from me;
> give me neither poverty nor riches,
> but give me only my daily bread.
> Otherwise, I may have too much and disown you
> and say, "Who is the LORD?"
> Or I may become poor and steal,
> and so dishonor the name of my God.

I find it so interesting that Lemuel prays for neither poverty *nor riches*. Many of us pray to avoid poverty, but I know of so few who pray not to be rich either! Instead, Lemuel asks for his daily bread only—what he needs to meet his most basic needs (not greeds!). He prays this because he knows either extreme—wealth or poverty—will lead him away from his God. If he is too poor, he may steal and bring dishonor to God; if he is too rich, he may see no more need for God. Lemuel points us toward the ideal income—enough to be comfortable, but not so much that money becomes a stumbling block to us. These are challenging verses, but I urge you to make Lemuel's prayer your own!

Honesty: Still the Best Policy

In adopting a healthy, biblical attitude towards money, we will want to make honesty a hallmark of all our financial dealings. Proverbs 28:6 makes our choice clear: "Better a poor man whose walk is blameless than a rich man whose ways are perverse." Far better to be poor and honest than rich and a scoundrel. So suppose you go to buy a soda for $1.27. You hand the cashier a five, so you should get $3.73 in change. The trouble is he thinks you gave him a ten, so he hands you back $8.73. The extra money would sure help your plans for this weekend. But at what cost? Remember, wealth cannot provide for your spiritual needs. Only a walk with God—which includes the "blameless walk"—can accomplish that. In other words, it would be better to give back the extra $5 and get the interest in your spiritual banking account than to put it in your wallet—and thereby make an unnecessary deduction from your spiritual savings.

Three proverbs will help us get a better feel for how we can avoid dishonesty in our financial transactions. First, Proverbs 11:1 notes, "The LORD abhors dishonest scales, but accurate weights are his delight." This proverb carries us back to Ancient Near Eastern business practices, as few of us use scales when making purchases anymore. The idea is, suppose someone wants to buy a pound of wheat. An honest seller will have a scale that weighs out the correct amount. But a dishonest seller will have a scale that is too light, so that he only has to give three quarters of a pound of wheat instead of the full pound. We can update this proverb for today by simply saying we should be honest in whatever business we find ourselves in, whether that would be calculating our tax return, giving change back to our parents after a textbook purchase, or selling our old guitar to an acquaintance. The temptation to cheat and take money that isn't ours is overwhelming. But remember, the Lord hates dishonesty in this area.

Second, if we must be honest in our private money matters, we must also work for honesty in public affairs as well. Proverbs 13:23 says, "A poor man's field may produce abundant food, but injustice sweeps it away." Corruption exists everywhere in the world. People are desperate for money (they never learned the ideal income), and so they cheat and steal from whomever they can. Sometimes this happens at the government level or with very large businesses. As Christians we must be aware that injustice takes place, and whenever possible, we must work to overcome it. We must also refuse to participate in such injustices. Suppose you work for a company that has been "cooking the books." If you are aware of this practice, your conscience should lead you to confront those in charge or leave the company, if need be.

Lastly, in seeking to be honest, we should be willing to go above and beyond what is expected of us if we are able to. Proverbs 3:27–28 says, "Do not withhold good from those who deserve it, / when it is in your power to act. / Do not say to your neighbor, 'Come back later; I'll give it tomorrow'—when you now have it with you." If you buy your friend's old guitar and promise to pay her by the end of the month, pay her as soon as you get the money—even if it's before the end of the month. There is no reason to keep the money from her if you already have it. Or, if your parents give you $40 to fill up the car with gas, and it only costs $30, give them the ten dollars back. Most of us would prefer to keep the $10 for later, but Proverbs teaches us not to withhold good from those who deserve it.

Thinking about the Poor

We already saw above the need to keep ourselves from any economic injustice, which usually takes place against the poor. Now we're going to take a step back and look at how we should think about the poor generally.

Indeed, even thinking about *how to think about* the poor is a good start. Proverbs 29:7 says, "The righteous care about justice for the poor, but the wicked have no such concern." Righteous people—wise people—care about the poor and think about how to better their lot. The wicked don't even give it a second thought. In the city where I live, I am constantly surrounded by abject poverty. Many of my students consistently demonstrate a deep concern for the plight of these people. But some seem to have forgotten the suffering that takes place just down the street from them. Whether you live in an affluent area or not, I hope you will not forget the poor around you—and that you will pay them a second thought.

Of course, a proper perspective on the poor includes more than just thinking about them. We must also work to ensure that they do get justice. Proverbs 31:8-9 tells us, "Speak up for those who cannot speak for themselves, / for the rights of all who are destitute. / Speak up and judge fairly; defend the rights of the poor and needy." Whenever possible, we must stand up for those who cannot stand for themselves. In many cases today, these issues have become confused by political machinations. I don't want to dive too deeply into politics because the lines get blurred quickly. But whatever your political orientation—now or in the future—I hope you will bring a concern for global poverty into your consideration. I have two very good friends, colleagues at my school. One is deeply, deeply liberal on economic issues, and the other as strongly conservative. What impresses me about both is that in *each case* my friends have made their political decisions because of a desire to help the poor—in Colombia, in the United States, and across the globe.

In contrast to my friends are the many people who never even consider the poor when making decisions—political or personal. In today's world, it is impossible to remain unaware of the poverty that afflicts many regions on nearly every continent. Still, some pay no attention to this suffering. They have effectively deafened their ears to the cries of the needy because if they listened, their lives would have to change. They could not spend money on frivolous items—MP3 players and laptops, luxury cars, designer clothing, even designer coffees—knowing their brothers and sisters around the world were starving. And so they shut themselves off from this suffering. To such people the Lord says, "If a man shuts his ears to the cry of the poor, he too will cry out and not be answered" (Proverbs 21:13). Deaf ears always reflect a hard heart, and the Lord responds harshly to those who harden their hearts. (In fact, seeing if you care about the poor can be a good way to test how hard or soft your heart is.)

As if it weren't bad enough that the Lord stop listening to you if you stop listening to the cries of the poor, it gets worse. Proverbs 22:22–23 says, "Do not exploit the poor because they are poor / and do not crush the needy in court, / for the LORD will take up their case / and will plunder those who plunder them." That's a frightening thought. See, the Lord often chooses sides—and almost without fail, he chooses the side of the poor. If you're on the side that's exploiting the poor (which includes being the kid who wastes his money on frivolous luxuries instead of helping others), the Lord chooses sides against you. Those who steal from the poor will get plundered in the end. After all, you can't take your money with you, and you *sure* shouldn't expect to see it in heaven if you got it in unrighteous ways!

One final proverb shows us why it matters so much to God whether you are kind or cruel towards the poor. Proverbs 14:31 says, "He who oppresses the poor shows contempt for their Maker, but whoever is kind to the needy honors God." We must care for the poor precisely because *God is their Creator*—their Maker—and as human beings created in his image, they have a right to the same dignity as every other human. By treating the image of God in humanity poorly, those who oppress the poor dishonor God. In contrast, those who see in every human the divine spark, and who therefore help raise all people up to a level above poverty, honor God. So how we treat the poor is, in effect, how we treat God. With this in mind, let's look at the last area—giving—to see what it means to be "kind to the needy."

Lending to the Lord

We've now learned the proper attitude towards the poor—but of course this is an attitude that needs to be changed into action. The most important action is giving—being willing to support relief efforts for the poor around the world, and in your backyard. Proverbs 19:17 says, "He who is kind to the poor lends to the LORD, and he will reward him for what he has done." God's honor is at stake with the poor, because, after all, he made them. So in a sense, by giving to the poor, one is lending to the Lord. I think this idea raises charity to a whole new level, don't you? I mean, if Jesus came to you today and asked you to spot him $10, who among us would say no, especially in light of all he has done for us? I would do all I could to show my gratitude to the Lord in even the tiniest way for his work on the cross for me. Paul says in Romans 8:32, "He who did not spare his own Son, but gave him up for us all—how will he not also, along with him, graciously give us all things?" If God has given us all that in Christ, what should we give him in return? How can we show him our grateful love? In this proverb, the Lord tells us how: by lending to the poor. And the amazing thing is that God himself will take on the debt, promising to repay us for our loan! (I guess that means we shouldn't make the poor pay us back—the Lord will take care of it at another day!)

This is not the only proverb that promises reward to those who give. Several others all make the same point. The smartest financial choice you can make is to start giving to the poor, because then the Lord himself will promise to repay you (whether in this life or the next—and personally, I'd rather it were the next!). Proverbs 11:25 says, "A generous man will prosper; he who refreshes others will himself be refreshed." The phrase "a generous man" reads literally "one bestowing blessing," referring to our whole duty to the poor—including giving and prayer. Such people will receive full satisfaction—as much from their good deeds as from any reward that comes. The second half of the proverb promises that those who "drench" others (think of watering a crop) will themselves get soaked.[2]

I have seen this happen many times in my own life. As missionaries, my wife and I are very rarely in possession of much extra income. Still, we're surrounded by such need that we have at times given beyond what we can really afford to give. Recently, for example, we purchased school supplies for four children in our church—at a cost of several hundred dollars. While this gift hurt us financially, the next month we received more support than we usually do. We did our best to refresh someone else, and we were refreshed as a result. (I don't share this to boast about our giving habits but so that you can see that the promises of God are true in Christ Jesus.)

This happens the other way too. Those who give a blessing receive a blessing; but those who withhold their blessing often find themselves cursed instead. Proverbs 28:27 says, "He who gives to the poor will lack nothing, but he who closes his eyes to them receives many curses." Those who do not give can still expect to receive—only they will receive punishment in many ways instead. When hardships come, as they inevitably do, people will usually respond first to the generous. They may never give to someone who never gave to them. In Charles Dickens' classic, *A Christmas Carol*, no one cared for Scrooge when he died in his vision, because he had never cared for anyone else. Plus, those who are stingy never experience the profound joy that comes from helping someone else, even at great cost to themselves. And that is a curse in and of itself.

I know that hardly any teenagers have enough money to do much giving, but I also know that almost all teenagers have some money—whether from an allowance or a part-time job. Now is the time to establish a good pattern of sacrificial giving in your life. Search out ways to help the poor in your community or across the globe. You could consider doing a fundraiser for refugees of war or the homeless in your neighborhood. Many organizations (like World Vision and Compassion International) allow you to sponsor a child monthly at an affordable rate—maybe $20 a month. However you do it, find ways to bless those who need your blessing now. Starting at a young age will help you to become a cheerful giver so that when you're older and richer, you continue in your work of blessing others.

Memory Verse

"Give me neither poverty nor riches, but give me only my daily bread."
Proverbs 30:8b

Study Questions

1. How important is money to you? How important do you think it should be?

2. What are some things that are worth more than money to you?

3. Do you think Lemuel was wise to pray as he did? Why or why not?

4. What are some ways you may be tempted to be dishonest with your money now? How could you be above reproach in those situations?

5. Do you often think about poverty around the world? What are some ways you could work to battle against it?

THIRTEEN

LEAVING A LEGACY

In the final chapter of this book, I want to apply all that we have learned to the notion of leaving a legacy. At the culmination of our lives, people will look back on all that we have done, and a memory—an impression—will form. This is our legacy. Our kids, our friends, even our enemies—everyone will remember the tenor of our lives, whether good or bad. What I want to suggest to you in this chapter is that you have already begun to shape your legacy. Even now, every choice you make will shape the impression people will have of you. Choose for yourself this day: will you strive to leave a positive or negative legacy when you leave this earth?

FOR EVERY ACTION...

Newton's Third Law of Motion states that for every action there is an equal and opposite reaction. This holds true not just in the realm of physics but in our choices too. When we act, consequences inevitably follow. In a sense, everything we have talked about so far in this book is an application of this principle. How you make decisions will have consequences. Your choices about sex will have consequences. Your speech, your work ethic, your use of money will all have consequences. The question is: Are you willing to think of the consequences when making these choices?

In a pattern we've seen many times before, Proverbs compares the consequences of being wicked or righteous twice in chapter eleven. First, "The righteousness of the blameless makes a straight way for them, but the wicked are brought down by their own wickedness" (11:5). The blameless—those who try to lead righteous lives—have an easier time getting where they're going, presumably to God's dwelling place. The wicked, contrarily, stumble over their own wickedness. Wickedness, in this metaphor, proves to be an obstacle on an otherwise empty highway. This verse states in a general way what we have seen in specific ways over and over again: actions have consequences, and those consequences will harm the wicked and benefit the righteous.

Second, "The wicked man earns deceptive wages, but he who sows righteousness reaps a sure reward" (11:18). Here Proverbs pictures the wicked person as a worker, laboring for some wage. Unfortunately, she never earns what she desires. People who try to enjoy sex outside of God's blessing—outside of marriage—end up enjoying it far less. People who cheat to get ahead often find themselves flunking or fired. In other words, the consequences for the wicked are never what they hope—always worse. On the other hand, the righteous earn exactly the wages they seek. The metaphor of a farmer emphasizes the certainty of the reward: if you plant seed, you will reap a crop. Similarly, if you "plant" righteousness, you will reap a sure reward. Consequences will come whether you choose evil or good. The choice should be easy, however. Choosing good means a smooth highway leading to certain reward; choosing evil means stumbling into harm you never expected.

The Legacy You Leave

Consequences stack up and the resulting pile will be your legacy. In two more sets of contrasts, Proverbs propels us irresistibly towards choosing well. Your choices in life will determine ultimately the *memory of your name* and the *future of your hopes*—in a word, your legacy.

The Memory of Your Name

What's in a name? Why do our names matter? A person's name carries with it the memory of that person—what he accomplished, what she stood for, what horrors they committed. If I were to mention Martin Luther King Jr., you might think of justice and peaceful protest. To mention Adolf

Hitler, however, would surely call to mind the Holocaust, evil and atrocity such as the world has never seen. A name matters so much to some people because they recognize that it attaches to their memory. In Arthur Miller's *The Crucible*—a play about the Salem Witch Trials—John Proctor signs a false confession, saying he engaged in witchcraft. When the judge asks for it, to post it in the town, he refuses—and as a result is hanged! When asked why he wouldn't give the confession to the judge, he says, "Because it is my name! Because I cannot have another in my life!" Proctor understood that the memory of a name endures.

So what do people think of when they hear your name? Do they think kind or cruel? Selfish or loving? Proud or humble? Our choices in life will determine the memory of our names. Proverbs 10:7 warns, "The memory of the righteous will be a blessing, but the name of the wicked will rot." If your choices have been good, if you have zealously pursued righteousness, your memory will bless others. Probably this refers to the act of blessing someone else, as in Ruth 4:12, "May your family be like that of Perez, whom Tamar bore to Judah." Wouldn't it be great to have the memory of your name associated so closely with some positive characteristic that people blessed others with your name? Imagine, "May you be as kind as Amy," or "May you be as loyal as Marty." But what of those who pursue wickedness instead of righteousness? Their names will rot. The only memory people will have of them will be of their evil. As Shakespeare said in *Julius Caesar*, "The evil that men do lives after them; the good is oft interred with their bones." Probably Proverbs intends to compare the wicked person's name with a decaying body—neither will last very long after death. Better to be a blessing, I would think.

The Bible gives us a classic example of remembering the names of good people while the name of an evil man is left to rot. Some four hundred years after Joseph's rise to prominence in Egypt, a new Pharaoh takes the throne—one who does not remember Joseph. He begins to oppress the Hebrew people and—because they were becoming so numerous—orders two midwives to kill every Hebrew boy that is born. However, these two Hebrew midwives disobeyed the Pharaoh and spared the lives of the Hebrew boys. Amazingly, the Bible does not record this pharaoh's name—it has been left to rot. But the memory of these righteous women has been a blessing to many since then: their "names were Shiphrah and Puah" (Exodus 1:15). Now, you probably didn't remember their names off the top of your head, and I suspect few Christians could. But if you're reading through your Bible every year (as you should!), then once a year you come to these great women. Imagine all of the millions of Christians worldwide reading the names of these great women in hundreds of languages every single year. Contrast that with the handful of Egyptologists who know the name of the pharaoh who gave the horrid command. How will people remember you—as the nameless pharaoh or the courageous midwives?

Even in life a name matters. Proverbs 22:1 notes, "A good name is more desirable than great riches; to be esteemed is better than silver or gold." When considering major purchases, I often ask the question, "What's worth more than money?" Here Proverbs tells us that a good name is. I am often amazed at how flippantly some people treat their names. They will sign contracts (with their names) and then promptly break them. They will give their word and then fail to keep it. Some will even boast in sin—promiscuous sex, illegal activity, outright cruelty—so that others have no choice but to think poorly of them. Such people consider esteem to be of little consequence. But Proverbs tells us otherwise. A good name matters because the name you forge in life will be the memory you leave in death. You're going to leave a legacy—make sure it's a good one.

The Future of Your Hopes

Hope springs eternal, as the saying goes. All people have hopes—plans for their future that they want to see come to pass. Many of these hopes extend beyond our lifetimes. I know I have hopes for all of my kids—and I only have one so far! But I hope already for their future—for their marriages, for their children, for their service to God—and these hopes will last long after I am gone. Part of the legacy that we will leave relates to these hopes. Proverbs 10:28 says, "The prospect of the righteous is joy, but the hopes of the wicked come to nothing." As righteous men and women, we have the prospect of joy—unending joy in the presence of our God in heaven. I hope for nothing quite so much as I hope for this. But this is not the only way our hopes will be fulfilled. Many of my other hopes—such as accomplishing the tasks God has given me, or seeing some of my loved ones come to Christ—I am assured will come to fruition because God stands behind them. In contrast stand the wicked, whose hopes come to nothing. Not only do they not have the hope of heaven, but other hopes—such as leaving a mark on the world—will often fall flat.

Indeed, Proverbs tells us elsewhere that the wicked man's hopes will not come to anything: "When a wicked man dies, his hope perishes; all he expected from his power comes to nothing" (Proverbs 11:7). The wicked seek to create pleasure for themselves, but once death comes, they can preserve their pleasure no longer. As one scholar puts it, "the wicked hope to retain their present pleasures, but their expectation will end in a dying gasp… because what they delight in is inconsistent with the character of the Holy One who holds the future."[1] At the point of death, we all will lack the power to change our hopes; our legacy will be set. The question then will be did we live in such a way that our hopes will be met or not?

Conclusion

Not only in this chapter but throughout this book—and throughout the book of Proverbs—we are given a choice: wisdom or folly. Each bears certain consequences, and how we choose will determine our legacy. I leave you with this choice now—not altogether unlike the choice Joshua gave the Israelites once they had entered the Promised Land: "Choose for yourselves this day whom you will serve, whether the gods your forefathers served beyond the River, or the gods of the Amorites, in whose land you are living. But as for me and my household, we will serve the LORD" (Joshua 24:15). I hope you will choose as Joshua did—to serve the Lord, to follow the path of wisdom—knowing that it is for the best. To aid you in your choice, I leave you with two final thoughts—the two ways contrasted one last time.

The foolish persist in foolishness. Fools go down to the grave, and yet never stop to wonder if they should change direction. Proverbs 26:11 mocks this carelessness, "As a dog returns to its vomit, so a fool repeats his folly." Dogs—not being the brightest creatures on God's green earth (I'm a cat person)—sometimes eat their own vomit. We, as highly intelligent beings, don't normally do this. And yet so often we do so much worse, by repeating foolish choices throughout our lives. People get fired from several jobs for the same irresponsibility. Others get caught driving while intoxicated several times before going to jail or losing their licenses. Men and women both continue in relationships—sexual or not—that bring them nothing but heartache and a lack of fulfillment. Teenagers destroy friendship after friendship with needless, hurtful gossip. And no one changes.

Make today the day to change. "The fear of the Lord is the beginning of wisdom, and knowledge of the Holy One is understanding" (Proverbs 9:10). There is much wisdom contained in Proverbs. Apply it to your life—drink deeply from this well of understanding—and grow closer to God as a result. Nothing but folly will keep you from the knowledge of God. Fear the Lord and start to grow wise.

Memory Verse

"The memory of the righteous will be a blessing, but the name of the wicked will rot."
Proverbs 10:7

Study Questions

1. What does Newton's Third Law of Motion have to do with leaving a positive spiritual legacy?

2. What might people think of when they hear your name? What do you want them to think of? Try to think of at least three traits.

3. What do you hope for? What assurance do you have that those hopes will come true?

4. One last time, how will you choose—wisdom or folly? Christ or the world?

Notes

Chapter Four

1. Elisabeth Elliot, *Discipline: The Glad Surrender* (Grand Rapids: Revell, 1982), 17.
2. Bruce K. Waltke, *The Book of Proverbs: Chapters 15–31* (Grand Rapids: Eerdmans, 2005), 459 (emphasis added).

Chapter Five

1. Bruce K. Waltke, *The Book of Proverbs: Chapters 15–31* (Grand Rapids: Eerdmans, 2005), 233.

Chapter Six

1. *Proverbs 1-9: A New Translation with Introduction and Commentary* (New York: Doubleday, 2000), 199.
2. Wendy Shalit, *A Return to Modesty: Discovering the Lost Virtue* (New York: Touchstone, 1999), 171.

Chapter Seven

1. Bruce K. Waltke, *The Book of Proverbs: Chapters 15-31* (Grand Rapids: Eerdmans, 2005), 383.

Chapter Eight

1. John S. Feinberg, *No One Like Him* (Wheaton, IL: Crossway, 2001), 32.

Chapter Twelve

1. Bruce K. Waltke, *The Book of Proverbs: Chapters 1-15* (Grand Rapids: Eerdmans, 2004), 627.
2. Ibid., 507-508.

Chapter Thirteen

1. Bruce K. Waltke, *The Book of Proverbs: Chapters 1-15* (Grand Rapids: Eerdmans, 2004), 478.